C000134450

365

Churches, Abbeys and Cathedrals

visit**Britain**

Information
at your fingertips

When it comes to having a great day out, there's no finer place than England. This pocket guide is brimming with a wide selection of churches, abbeys and cathedrals, each one offering something of special interest to the visitor. Whatever your religious belief, you are bound to be humbled by the experience of visiting one of the many fascinating places of worship around the English regions – from the majesty of Canterbury Cathedral to the intimacy of Whalley Parish Church. Dip into this guide and you'll find 365 places of worship that welcome visitors, one for every day of the year!

The attractions in this guide are alphabetically ordered by county, and then by town. Some attractions will be accompanied by the following symbol:

The Quality Assured Visitor Attraction sign indicates that the attraction is assessed annually and meets the standards required to receive the quality marque.

Key to attraction facilities	
☕	Café/restaurant
◌	Picnic area
🐕	Dogs allowed
🐕	No dogs except service dogs
♿	Full disabled access
♿ᴾ	Partial disabled access

How to use this guide

Each visitor attraction contains the following essential information.

① ③ ④ ②

Canterbury Cathedral

CANTERBURY

Canterbury Cathedral, The Precincts, Canterbury, CT1 2EH
t: (01227) 762862   **w:** canterbury-cathedral.org

open: All year, Mon-Sat 0900-1700, Sun 1230-1400.
admission: £5.50

description: Founded in AD597, it is the Mother Church of Anglican Communion and has a Romanesque crypt, 12thC Gothic quire and 14thC nave. Site of Thomas Becket's murder in AD1170.

facilities:

⑤ ⑦ ⑥

1   Name
2   City/Town
3   Address and contact details
4   Opening times
5   Price of admission
6   Description
7   Facilities

Admission is free if the price is not specified. The price is based on a single adult admission.

Please note, as changes often occur after press date, it is advisable to confirm opening times and admission prices before travelling.

John Bunyan Museum and Bunyan Meeting Free Church

BEDFORD

The John Bunyan Museum and Bunyan Meeting Free Church, Mill Street, Bedford, MK40 3EU   **t:** (01234) 213722

open: Church: all year, Tue-Sat 1000-1600. Museum: Mar-Oct, Tue-Sat 1100-1545.

description: The church where John Bunyan was once minister. Includes a museum housing his personal effects and copies of The Pilgrim's Progress in over 170 languages, together with other works.

facilities: 🍵 ♿ ♿

Bushmead Priory

COLMWORTH

Bushmead Priory, Colmworth, MK44 2LD
t: (01799) 522842   **w:** english-heritage.org.uk

open: May-Aug, Pre-booked guided tours only.
admission: £5.00

description: A small Augustinian priory founded c1195 with a magnificent 13thC timber roof of crown-post construction. There are also medieval wall paintings and stained glass.

facilities: ♿ ♿

Elstow Abbey

ELSTOW

Elstow Abbey, Church End, Elstow, MK42 9XT
t: (01234) 261477   w: elstow-abbey.org.uk

open: Please contact keyholder on (01234) 218762.

description: Former Benedictine nunnery founded in 1078 by the niece of William the Conqueror. Six Norman arches still remain. Elstow is famous as the home of writer and preacher John Bunyan.

facilities: 🐕 ⛪ ♿

Jordans Meeting House

BEACONSFIELD

Jordans Meeting House, Welders Lane, Jordans, Beaconsfield, HP9 2SN   t: (01494) 675280
w: quakers-chilterns-area.org.uk

open: Please contact Meeting House for details.

description: In the 17th century Jordans Farm was a meeting place of the early Quakers including William Penn, founder of Pennsylvania. Major rebuilding was needed following a fire in 2005.

facilities: 🚶 ♿

Buckingham Chantry Chapel

BUCKINGHAM

Buckingham Chantry Chapel, Market Hill, Buckingham, MK18 1JX   **t:** (01280) 823020   **w:** nationaltrust.org.uk

open: Please phone for details.

description: Chapel rebuilt in 1475 still retains a fine Norman doorway. Restored by Sir George Gilbert Scott in 1875.

facilities:

Saint Lawrence Church

MILTON KEYNES

St Lawrence Church, Broughton Village, Milton Keynes, MK10 9AA   **t:** (020) 7213 0660   **w:** visitchurches.org.uk

open: Please phone for details.

description: St Lawrence seems an unexceptional 14thC church with an elegant 15thC tower, but inside is a marvellous series of wall paintings found during an 1849 restoration.

facilities:

Saint Giles Church
Thomas Gray The Poet's Burial Place

STOKE POGES

St Giles Church Thomas Gray The Poet's Burial Place,
Church Lane, Stoke Poges, SL2 4PE
t: (01753) 521778   **w:** stokepogeschurch.org

open: Apr-Sep, Daily 0900-1700. Oct-Mar, Daily
0930-1530.

description: Norman church and the burial place of the
poet Thomas Gray. Associations with the Penn
family of Pennsylvania.

facilities: 🐕 ♿

Cambridge All Saints

CAMBRIDGE

Cambridge All Saints, Jesus Lane, Cambridge, CB5 8BS
t: (020) 7213 0660   **w:** visitchurches.org.uk

open: Please phone for details.

description: This spire of this fine
Victorian church is
a prominent local
landmark. The interior
is a milestone of the
Gothic revival, with
richly painted stencil
wall decoration and
stained glass by William
Morris and other Pre-Raphaelites.

facilities: 🐕 ♿

Kings College Chapel

Kings College Chapel, Kings College, Cambridge,
CB2 1ST   **t:** (01223) 331212   **w:** kings.cam.ac.uk

open:	Term Time: Mon-Fri 0930-1530, Sat 0930-1515, Sun 1315-1415. School Hols: Mon-Sat 0930-1630, Sun 1000-1700.
admission:	£4.50

description: The chapel, founded by Henry VI, includes the breathtaking fan-vault ceiling, stained glass windows, a carved oak screen and Ruben's masterpiece The Adoration of the Magi.

facilities:

Ely Cathedral

Ely Cathedral, Chapter House, The College, Ely, CB7 4DL
t: (01353) 667735   **w:** cathedral.ely.anglican.org

open: Apr-Oct, daily 0700-1900. Nov-Mar, Mon-Sat 0730-1800, Sun 0730-1700.
admission: £5.20

description: One of England's finest cathedrals with guided tours and tours of the Octagon and West Tower and monastic precincts. Also a brass-rubbing centre and The Stained Glass Museum.

facilities:

Saint Michael's Church

LONGSTANTON

St Michael's Church (Thatched), St Michaels Road,
Longstanton, CB4 5BZ   **t:** (020) 7213 0660
w: visitchurches.org.uk

open: All year, Sun 1400-1600. Please contact keyholder for access at other times.

description: An adorable small village church with a double bell cote and thatched roof. It has a superb 13thC double piscina, with its two drains set beneath intersecting arches.

facilities:

Saint Wendreda's Church

MARCH

Saint Wendreda's Church, Church Street, March
t: (01354) 654783   **w:** stwendreda.co.uk

open: All year, daily. Please contact keyholder for access.

description: This church is noted for its exceptional double hammerbeam timber roof which contains 120 carved angels.

facilities:

Peterborough Cathedral

PETERBOROUGH

Peterborough Cathedral, 12a Minster Precincts,
Peterborough, PE1 1XS **t:** (01733) 343342
w: peterborough-cathedral.org.uk

open:	All year, Mon-Fri 0900-1830, Sat 0900-1700, Sun 0730-1700.
admission:	£3.50
description:	A Norman cathedral with an Early English west front, a 13thC painted nave ceiling and the tomb of Catherine of Aragon. It was also the former burial place of Mary Queen of Scots.
facilities:	

Thorney Abbey Church

PETERBOROUGH

Thorney Abbey Church, Thorney, Peterborough, PE6 0QD
t: (01733) 270 420   **w:** thorneyabbey.co.uk

open:	Daily.
description:	Abbey church with a Norman nave, c1100, a fine church organ originally built in 1787-1790, and a stained glass east window depicting the miracles of St Thomas Becket.
facilities:	

Saint Ives Bridge Chapel

ST IVES

Saint Ives Bridge Chapel, Bridge Street, St Ives, PE27 5EP
t: (01480) 497314

open:	May-Sep, Mon-Sat 100-1700, Sun 1400-1700. Oct-Apr, Mon-Fri 1000-1600, Sat 1000-1300.
description:	A 15thC chapel built onto the bridge, in midstream. One of only four of its kind in England. With balcony over the river.
facilities:	🐕 ♿

Chester Cathedral

CHESTER

Chester Cathedral, St Werburgh Street, Chester,
CH1 2HU   **t:** (01244) 324756
w: chestercathedral.com

open:	All year, Mon-Sat 0900-1700, Sun 1300-1700.
admission:	£4.00

description: A 14thC-15thC cathedral. The 12thC monastic building has a magnificent refectory, and the church has spectacular carved choir stalls. Each visitor receives an audio tour.

facilities: 💻 🍴 ⛱ ♿

All Saints Church

All Saints Church, Daresbury Lane, Daresbury, WA4 4AE
t: (01925) 740348   **w:** daresburycofe.org.uk

open: Apr-Sep 0900-1800, Oct-Mar 0900-1600.

description: All Saints Church in Daresbury features a 16thC font, 17thC pulpit and a memorial window to Lewis Carroll who was born in the village.

facilities: 🐕 ♿

Parish Church of St Mary

Parish Church of St Mary, Nantwich, CW5 5RQ
t: (01270) 625268   **w:** stmarysnantwich.btinternet.co.uk

open: Apr-Oct, Mon-Fri 0830-1730, Nov-Mar, Mon-Fri 0830-1600.

description: A 13thC building known as the 'Cathedral of South Cheshire'. Fine architectural features include modern needlework, glass and medieval wood carvings.

facilities: ☕ 🐕 ♿

Norton Priory Museum and Gardens

RUNCORN

Norton Priory Museum and Gardens, Tudor Road, Manor Park, Runcorn, WA7 1SX
t: (01928) 569895   w: nortonpriory.org

Open: Apr-Oct, Mon-Fri 1200-1700, Sat-Sun 1200-1800. Nov-Mar, daily 1200-1600.

Admission: £4.95

Description: Medieval priory remains, purpose-built museum, St Christopher's statue, sculpture trail and award-winning walled garden, all set in 38 acres of beautiful gardens.

Facilities: 🛏 🐕 🛋 ♿

Bristol Cathedral

BRISTOL

Bristol Cathedral, College Green, Bristol, BS1 5TJ
(0117) 926 4879   w: bristol-cathedral.co.uk

Open: Daily 0800-1730.

Description: Once an Augustinian abbey and splendid 12thC Norman chapter house. Magnificent 13thC and 14thC architecture.

Facilities: 🛏 🍽

Bristol St. John
the Baptist

BRISTO

Bristol St John the Baptist, Broad Street, Bristol, BS1 2EZ
t: (020) 7213 0660   **w:** visitchurches.org.uk

open: Daily, please phone for details.

description: The elegant perpendicular spire
of St John's rises above the Gothic city gate
and the interior of the church is impressively
tall and graceful. Also home to a fine
collection of monuments.

facilities:

Saint Mary Redcliffe
Church

BRISTO

St Mary Redcliffe Church, 10 Redcliffe
Parade West, Bristol, BS1 6SP
t: (0117) 929 1487
w: stmaryredcliffe.co.uk

open: Apr-Oct, Mon-Sat 0830-
                   1700, Sun 0800-1930.
                   Nov-Mar, Mon-Sat 0900-
                   1600, Sun 0800-1930.

description: One of the finest examples of Gothic
                   architecture in England. The north porch
                   is ornate Early English and the spire was
                   completed c1872.

facilities:

See pages 2-3 for key to symbols

New Room - John Wesley's Chapel

The New Room - John Wesley's Chapel, 36 The Horsefair, Bristol, BS1 3JE   **t:** (0117) 926 4740
w: newroombristol.org.uk

Open: All year, Mon-Sat 1000-1600.

Description: The oldest Methodist building in the world. Built as a meeting room and accommodation after Wesley began to preach in the open air in Bristol in 1739.

Facilities: � ⊨ 🛆 ⊼ ♿

Clifton Cathedral

Clifton Cathedral, Clifton Park, Clifton, BS8 3BX
(0117) 973 8411   **w:** cliftoncathedral.org.uk

Open: Daily 0730-1800.

Description: Modern Roman Catholic cathedral. The Cathedral was consecrated on 29 June 1973, replacing a wooden-framed pro-Cathedral that had been built in the mid-19th century.

Facilities: 🛆 ♿

PORTSCATHO

Roseland St Anthony's Church

Roseland St Anthony's Church, Roseland, Portscatho,
TR2 5EY   **t:** (020) 7213 0660   **w:** visitchurches.org.uk

open: Daily 1000-1630.

description: Picturesquely situated looking across the
                   creek to St Mawes, the church retains its
                   original medieval plan and appearance. It
                   also features notable Victorian work, and
                   impressive monuments to members of the
                   Spry family.

facilities: 🐕

TRURO

Truro Cathedral

Truro Cathedral, The Cathedral Office, 14 St Mary's Street,
Truro, TR1 2AF   **t:** (01872) 276782   **w:** trurocathedral.org.uk

open: All year, Mon-Sat 0730-1800, Sun 0900-1900.

description: Outstanding example of the
                   work of Victorian architect,
                   John Pearson, who favoured
                   the Gothic style, with strong
                   influences from French
                   churches.

facilities: 💺 🍴 ♿

Furness Abbey

Furness Abbey, Abbey Approach, Barrow-in-Furness,
LA13 0PJ   **t:** (01912) 691200   **w:** english-heritage.org.uk

open: See website for details.
admission: £3.40

description: A dramatic red sandstone abbey dating from 1123, so beloved by William Wordsworth. The exhibition explains the history of a powerful religious community.

facilities:

Lanercost Priory

Lanercost Priory, Lanercost, Brampton, CA8 2HQ
t: (01697) 73030   **w:** english-heritage.org.uk

open: See website for details.
admission: £2.70

description: Step back 800 years and explore this
                   wonderful 12thC Augustinian priory which is
                   situated near Hadrian's Wall.

facilities:

Carlisle Cathedral

Carlisle Cathedral, The Abbey, Carlisle, CA3 8TZ
t: (01228) 548151 **w:** carlislecathedral.org.uk

open:	All year, Mon-Sat 0730-1815, Sun 0730-1700.
description:	The cathedral dates from 1122 and has fine medieval stained glass, carved wood and stonework. Gift shop, restaurant, Treasury museum.
facilities:	☕ 🐕 ♿

Cartmel Priory

Cartmel Priory, Cartmel, Grange-over-Sands, LA11 6PU
t: (015395) 36261
w: cartmelpriory.org.uk

open: Apr-Sep, Daily 0900-1750, Oct-Mar, Daily 0900-1530.

description: Founded in 1189, Cartmel Priory Church shows three distinct architectural periods. There are many features of interest including the unique square belfry tower constructed diagonally across the original lantern tower.

facilities: 🏃 ♿

Shap Abbey

Shap Abbey, Shap, CA10 3NB
t: 0870 333 1181 **w:** english-heritage.org.uk

open: Daily.

description: The remains of a 12thC Premonstratensian
                 abbey including the foundations of the living
                 quarters and church. The striking 15thC West
                 Tower still stands to its original height.

facilities: 🐕 ♿

Conishead Priory House & Temple Tours

Conishead Priory House & Temple Tours, A5087 Coast Road,
Ulverston, LA12 9QQ   **t:** (01229) 584029
w: conisheadpriory.org

open: Jun-Oct, Sat-Sun, Bank Hols 1400-1700. Nov-
                 Mar, Sat-Sun 1400-1600.
admission: £2.50

description: A fascinating one-hour tour
                 giving the history of the
                 priory since 1160, together
                 with an insight into the
                 Buddhist way of life.

facilities: ☕ 🐕

ULVERSTON

Saint Mary & Saint Michael's Church

St Mary & St Michael's Church, Church Road, Great Urswick,
Ulverston, LA12 0TA   t: (01229) 582053

open: Apr-Oct, daily 1000-1600. Nov-Mar, daily
1000-1500.

description: A 10thC church, the oldest in Furness. Pre-Viking cross and Georgian gallery. Fine carvings by Alec Miller.

Possible Celtic, Roman connections.

facilities:

WINDERMERE

Parish Church of St Martin's

The Parish Church of St Martin's, Church Street, Bowness-on-Windermere, Windermere, LA23 3DG
t: (015394) 43063   w: stmartin.org.uk

open: Daily 1030-1630.

description: St Martin's is the ancient parish church for the whole of Windermere and believed to have been a site of Christian worship for over 1,100 years.

facilities:

Saint John's Chapel & Heritage Centre

St John's Chapel & Heritage Centre, St John's Chapel,
The Butts, Belper, DE56 1HX   **t:** (01773) 822116
w: belpertowncouncil.co.uk

open: Jan-Dec, Mon-Fri 0930-1230. Last Sat each
month 0930-1200

description: A stone chapel built c1250 with a heritage
centre containing historical details,
photographs and writings about Belper.

facilities:

Church of Saint Mary and Saint Hardulph

Church of Saint Mary and Saint Hardulph, Breedon on the
Hill, DE73 8AJ   **t:** (01332) 864845   **w:** benefice.org.uk

open: Daily 0900-1730.

description: A Norman church on a hilltop with fragments
of Saxon sculpture in the Mercian style built
into the structure and survivals from earlier
monastic buildings including the Breedon
Angel.

facilities:

Church of Saint Mary and All Saints

CHESTERFIELD

Church of Saint Mary and All Saints, Churchway,
Chesterfield, S40 1XJ   **t:** (01246) 206506
w: chesterfieldparishchurch.org.uk

open: Jan, Mon-Sat 0900-1500. Feb-Dec, Mon-Sat 0900-1700.

description: Well known for its crooked spire, the church dates from the 13th century with an interior containing rich furnishings.

facilities:

Chapel of St Mary on the Bridge

DERBY

Chapel of St Mary on the Bridge, Sowter Road, Derby,
DE1 3AT   **t:** (01332) 550422   **w:** derbycathedral.org

open: All year, Mon-Sat 0930-1700.

description: The medieval chapel, one of six remaining bridge chapels in England, was carefully restored in 1930, and is once more a thriving place of worship.

facilities:

Derby Cathedral & Derby Cathedral Centre

Derby Cathedral & Derby Cathedral Centre, 18/19 Iron Gate, Derby, DE1 3GP **t:** (01332) 341201 **w:** derbycathedral.org

open: Cathedral: Daily 0830-1800. Centre: Daily 0900-1700.

description: With its splendid medieval tower, historical monuments and thriving contemporary life, Derby Cathedral is at once a place of prayer and a unique visitor experience.

facilities:

Church of Saint Michael with Saint Mary

Church of Saint Michael with Saint Mary, Church Square, Melbourne, DE73 8JH **t:** (01332) 862347 **w:** melbourneparishchurch.com.uk

open: All year, Mon-Sat 0845-1730.

description: One of the finest Norman parish churches in Britain, a large cruciform building with nave pillars, carved arches, capitals and wall painting.

facilities:

Saint Lawrence Chapel (Old Grammar School)

ASHBURTON

St Lawrence Chapel (Old Grammar School), St Lawrence Lane, Ashburton, TQ13 7DD **t:** (01364) 653414
w: stlawrencechapel.ik.com

open: May-Sep, Tue, Thu-Sat 1400-1630.

description: A former chantry chapel and a grammar school, the chapel has long been the traditional meeting place of the Ancient Courts Leet and Baron.

facilities: 🐾 ♿

Buckfast Abbey

BUCKFASTLEIGH

Buckfast Abbey, Buckfastleigh, TQ11 0EE
t: (01364) 645500 **w:** buckfast.org.uk

open: All year, Mon-Thur 0900-1800, Fri 1000-1800, Sun 1200-1800.

description: Large Benedictine monastery rebuilt on medieval foundations. Many art treasures in the Abbey church. Also unusual shops, exhibition and excellent restaurant.

facilities: 🍽 🐾 ♿

Collegiate Church of the Holy Cross

The Collegiate Church of the Holy Cross, Church Street,
Crediton, EX17 2AH   **t:** (01363) 773226
w: creditonparishchurch.org.uk

open: All year, dawn-dusk.

description: Magnificent collegiate church on the site of Devon's first cathedral. Birthplace exposition of St Boniface, patron saint of Germany and the Netherlands.

facilities:

Loughwood Meeting House

Loughwood Meeting House, Dalwood, EX13 7DU
t: (01392) 881691   **w:** nationaltrust.org.uk

open: Daily 1000-1700.

description: Built c1653 by the Baptist congregation of
                   Kilmington. The interior, fitted in the early 18th
                   century, remains unaltered.

facilities:

Exeter Cathedral - Church of Saint Peter

Exeter Cathedral - Church of Saint Peter, The Cloisters,
Exeter, EX1 1HS   **t:** (01392) 255573
w: exeter-cathedral.org.uk

Open:	Daily 0930-1700.
Admission:	£3.50

Description:	Medieval cathedral. Fine example of Gothic Decorated style. Longest unbroken stretch of Gothic vaulting in the world.

Facilities:	🖥 ⚔ ⛫ ♿

Exeter St. Martin

Exeter St Martin, Cathedral Close, Exeter, EX1 1EZ
t: (020) 7213 0660   **w:** visitchurches.org.uk

Open:	All year, Mon-Fri 0930-1730, Sat 1000-1700.

Description:	The most important and complete church in the centre of Exeter. There has been a church on this site since 1065, and the present building combines an early-15thC remodelling with fine 18thC furnishings.

Facilities:	⚔

Saint Mary's Church

OTTERY ST MAR

St Mary's Church, The College, Ottery St Mary, EX11 1DQ
t: (01404) 812062   **w:** otterystmary.org.uk

open: See website for details.

description: Dating from the 13thC, the church was enlarged and modelled on Exeter Cathedral c1342. Given five star rating in 'England's Thousand Best Churches.'

facilities:

Parracombe, St. Petrock

PARRACOMB

Parracombe, St Petrock, Parracombe, EX31 4RA
t: (020) 7213 0660   **w:** visitchurches.org.uk

open: See website for details.

description: The modest medieval exterior of St Petrock's conceals a remarkable Georgian interior almost unchanged in 200 years, with wonderful 18thC fittings.

facilities:

orbryan Holy Trinity

orbryan Holy Trinity, Torbryan, TQ12 5UR
(020) 7213 0660   **w:** visitchurches.org.uk

pen:	Daily 1000-1600.
escription:	Church of considerable size and grandeur, with dramatic octagonal stair turret on the fine perpendicular tower. Also features a magnificent rood screen with delicate woodcarving spanning the full width of the interior.
cilities:	

aint Mary's Church

t Mary's Church, High Street, Totnes, TQ9 5NN
(01803) 866045   **w:** stmarystotnes.org.uk

pen:	See website for details.
escription:	This 15thC church contains many items of architectural interest including a 15thC stone screen, pulpit and font, 19thC Kempe window and Willis organ.
cilities:	

Saint Catherine's Chapel

ABBOTSBUR

St Catherine's Chapel, Abbotsbury
t: (01305) 820868   **w:** english-heritage.org.uk

open: All year, daily.

description: A small stone chapel, set on a
hilltop, with an unusual roof and
small turret previously used as
a lighthouse.

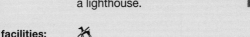

facilities: ✕

Christchurch Priory Church

CHRISTCHURCH

Christchurch Priory Church, Quay Road, Christchurch,
BH23 1BU   **t:** (01202) 485804   **w:** christchurchpriory.org

open: Apr-Oct, daily 0930-1700. Oct-Mar, daily
0930-1600.

description: Longest parish church in
England, dating from 1094. The west
tower can be climbed. Legendary
Miraculous Beam. Memorial to the poet
Shelley.

facilities: ✕ ⛺ ♿

ilton Abbey

lton Abbey, Milton Abbas, DT11 0BP
(01258) 880215   **w:** ruraldorset.com

en:	Daily 1000-1730.
mission:	£2.00
scription:	A 14thC abbey, church and abbots' hall. Gothic-style house.
cilities:	🐕 ♿

herborne Abbey

erborne Abbey, The Close, Sherborne, DT9 3LQ
(01935) 812452   **w:** sherborneabbey.com

en:	Apr-Oct, daily 0900-1800. Nov-Mar, daily 0900-1600.
scription:	Historic abbey church dating from Saxon times. Wealth of 15thC fan-vaulting built of hamstone. Fine monuments.
cilities:	♿

Stinsford Church

Stinsford Church, Church Lane, Stinsford, DT2 8PS
t: (01305) 267992

open: Daily 0900-1800.

description: Norman church with churchyard containing the graves of Thomas Hardy and the poet Cecil Day Lewis.

facilities: 🐕 ♿

Saint Mary the Virgin

St Mary the Virgin, Tarrant Crawford, DT11 9HU
t: (020) 7213 0660   **w:** visitchurches.org.uk

open: Daily, dawn-dusk.

description: This simple, unspoilt church stands on a slope above the River Tarrant. There is a series of 14thC paintings on the south wall.

facilities: 🐕 ♿

Wimborne Minster

Wimborne Minster, Church House, High Street, Wimborne Minster, BH21 1HT   **t:** (01202) 884753
w: wimborneminster.org.uk

Open:	Mar-Dec, daily 0930-1730. Jan-Feb, daily 0930-1600.

Description: Medieval church, Ethelred brass, astronomical clock, quarterjack, chained library and gift shop.

Facilities: 🏃 🪑 ♿

Saint Andrew's Church

St Andrew's Church, Off Marsh Lane, Winterborne Tomson, DT11 9HA   **t:** (01963) 824240   **w:** visitchurches.org.uk

Open: All year, daylight hours.

Description: Built of grey stone and flint with a small bell turret of board and tile, this small 11thC church is a delight. Repaired in 1931 using money raised from sale of Hardy manuscripts.

Facilities: 🏃 ♿

Egglestone Abbey

Egglestone Abbey, Barnard Castle, DL12 9TN
t: (01912) 691200   **w:** english-heritage.org.uk

open:	All year, Mon-Sun, Bank Hols 1000-1800.
description:	Picturesque ruins of Premonstratensian abbey Greater part of the nave and chancel still standing, with remains of cloistral buildings.
facilities:	

Escomb Saxon Church

Escomb Saxon Church, Escomb, Bishop Auckland,
DL14 7ST   **t:** (01388) 662265   **w:** escombsaxonchurch.com

open:	All year, Mon-Sun, Bank Hols 0900-2000.
description:	The Saxon church at Escomb is one of the finest in England. It dates to the 7thC and contains a Roman arch and stonework. For guided tours please ring in advance.
facilities:	

Saint Mary
Saint Cuthberts

CHESTER LE STREET

St Mary & St Cuthbert's, The Church Office, Parish Centre,
Church Chare, Chester Le Street, DH3 3QB
t: (0191) 3883295   **w:** maryandcuthbert.org.uk

open:	Apr-Oct, Mon-Wed, Fri-Sat 1000-1530, Thu 1300-1530. Nov-Mar, Mon-Fri 1000-1230. Closed at Christmas and New Year.
description:	A church with a fascinating history which starts in 883AD when monks from Lindisfarne built a shrine to Saint Cuthbert. The present building is 12thC with a 16thC two-storey anchorage.
facilities:	

Durham Cathedral

DURHAM

Durham Cathedral, The College, Durham,
DH1 3EH   **t:** (01913) 864266
w: durhamcathedral.co.uk

open:	Apr-Jul, Mon-Sat 0930-1800, Sun 0930-1730. Aug, daily 0930-2000. Sep-Mar, Mon-Sat 0930-1800, Sun 0930-1730.
description:	Durham Cathedral is thought by many to be the finest example of Norman church architecture in England. The cathedral contains the tombs of St Cuthbert and The Venerable Bede.
facilities:	

Finchale Priory

Finchale Priory, Brasside, Durham, DH9 5SH
t: (01913) 866528   **w:** english-heritage.org.uk

open:	Daily 0900-1700.
admission:	£2.50

description:	A 13thC Benedictine priory by the River Wear, built around the tomb of St Godric who lived in hermitage until he was 105.

facilities:

Weardale Museum and High House Chapel

Weardale Museum and High House Chapel, Ireshopeburn,
DL13 1EZ   **t:** (01388) 537417   **w:** weardalemuseum.co.uk

open: 21-24 Mar, Mon, Fri-Sun 1400-1700. May-Jul, Wed-Sun, Bank Hols 1400-1700. Aug, Mon-Sun, Bank Hols 1400-1700. Sep, Wed-Sun, Bank Hols 1400-1700.

admission:	£2.00

description:	High House Chapel is the oldest purpose-built Methodist chapel in the world in continuous weekly use since 1760. Includes a Wesley room, period cottage, local history and collection of minerals.

facilities:

Newbiggin Methodist Chapel

NEWBIGGIN IN TEESDALE

Newbiggin Methodist Chapel, Newbiggin in Teesdale,
DL12 0TY   t: (01325) 730985
w: enjoyengland.com/Attraction/Newbiggin-in-Teesdale

open: All year, Mon-Sun, Bank Hols 0900-1700.

description: Methodist chapel believed to be the oldest in
             continuous use and visited by John Wesley
             in the 1700s. Displays of Primitive Methodist
             material and lead mining information.

facilities: ⚒ ♿

Saint Mary the Virgin Church

OLD SEAHAM

St Mary the Virgin Church, Coast Road, Old Seaham,
SR7 7AG   t: (01915) 346492
w: enjoyengland.com/Attraction/Seaham

open: 1 Jun-12 Sep, Wed 1400-1600, Sat 1000-
             1600.

description: One of the finest small
             churches in the country.
             Late Saxon, early Norman
             nave, Elizabethan pulpit,
             Georgian box pews, late
             Saxon windows from the 7th or 8th centuries.

facilities: ⚑ ⎍ ♿

Saint Bartholomew's Church

St Bartholomew's Church, Church Street, Aldbrough, HU11 4RN **t:** (01964) 529032

open:	All year, Sat 1400-1600.
description:	An 11thC sundial in the south-aisle wall has an Anglo-Scandinavian inscription recording that Ulf built the church. The long narrow nave probably preserves the plan of Ulf's church. Also remains of two 11thC windows.
facilities:	

Saint Andrew's Church

St Andrew's Church, Church Street, Bainton, YO25 9NG **t:** (01377) 217622

open:	All year, Fri-Sun 0900-1700.
description:	An impressive church dating from c1330-1340 with a handsome tower that was once topped by a spire.
facilities:	

Beverley Minster

BEVERLEY

Beverley Minster, 38 Highgate, Beverley, HU17 0DN
t: (01482) 868540

open: Apr-Jul, Mon-Sat 0900-1700, Sun 1200-1630. Aug, Mon-Sat 0900-1730, Sun 1200-1630. Sep-Oct, Mon-Sat 0900-1700, Sun 1200-1630. Nov-Mar, Mon-Sat, 0900-1600, Sun 1200-1630.

description: A splendid example of medieval Gothic architecture, built 1220-1400. Well known for the Percy tomb, burial place of St John of Beverley, Saxon sanctuary chair and large collection of misericords.

facilities: ⚔ ♿

Bridlington Priory
St Marys Parish Church

BRIDLINGTON

Bridlington Priory St Marys Parish Church, Church Green, Bridlington, YO16 7JX
t: (01262) 601938   w: bridlingtonpriory.co.uk

open: May-Sep, Mon-Fri 1100-1600, Sat 1000-1200, Sun 1400-1600. Oct-Apr Mon-Sat 1000-1200.

description: Large ancient church, part of former priory. Pre-Reformation, but with later decoration and furnishing. Fine organ. Shop and exhibition of local history. Many interesting windows (the largest west window in the north of England).

facilities: ⚔ ♿

Saint Michael's Church

St Michael's Church, Church Lane, Catwick, HU17 5PW
t: (01964) 503731

open:	Please contact keyholder on (01964) 542128.
description:	A church at Catwick was mentioned in the Domesday Book, 1086. The present church, apart from the tower, dates from 1862-3 but incorporates medieval material, notably the reused chancel arch.
facilities:	🐕 ♿

Saint Peter's Church

St Peter's Church, Rowley, Little Weighton, Cottingham, HU20 3XR   t: (01482) 843317

open:	Daily.
description:	In 1638 the Puritan rector, the Revd Ezekiel Rogers, and many of his congregation, went to America where they founded Rowley, Massachusetts.
facilities:	🐕

GARTON-ON-THE-WOLDS

Church of St Michael and All Angels

The Church of St Michael and All Angels, Station Road, Garton-on-the-Wolds, YO25 3EX   **t:** (01377) 217622

open: Daily 0700-1800.

description: An imposing Norman church dating from around 1120. It was restored by Pearson for Tatton Sykes I in 1856-7, when he reconstructed the Norman south doorway and the chancel.

facilities: 🐕 ♿

HARPHAM

Church of St John of Beverley

The Church of St John of Beverley, Harpham, YO25 4NE
t: (01262) 490217

open: All year, daily 0900-1700.

description: A delightful church, full of interest, dedicated to St John of Beverley who is said to have been born in the village.

facilities: 🐕 ♿

Howden Minster

Howden Minster, Howden, DN14 7BL
t: (01430) 432056   **w:** howdenminster.net

open: Daily 0900-1700.

description: A large, partly-
                   ruined collegiate
                   minster church
                   dating from
                   the 13th-15th
                   centuries. Fine
                   nave and tower,
                   ruined choir and chapter house.

facilities: 🐾 ♿

Saint Mary's Church

St Mary's Church, Kirkburn, YO25 9DL
t: (01377) 217622

open: All year, Fri-Sun 0900-1700.

description: An early 12thC Norman church restored by
                   Pearson for Tatton Sykes I in 1856-7 when
                   the south porch was added. The spectacular
                   Norman doorway of three orders has
                   beakhead and zigzag in the arch.

facilities: 🐕 ♿

Saint Martin's Church

St Martin's Church, Lowthorpe, YO25 4AS
: (01262) 490217

open: All year, daily 0900-1700.

description: A most unusual church with a tall ruined chancel, the remnant of the collegiate church served by a rector and six chantry priests, founded in 1333 and dissolved in 1548.

facilities: ⚔ ♿

All Saints Church

All Saints Church, Church Street, North Cave, HU15 2GJ
: (01430) 470716

open: Apr-Oct, Thu 1330-1530, Keyholder nearby call (01430) 470716

description: Excellent stained glass by leading artists including Kempe, R Anning Bell and Douglas Strachan.

facilities: ☕ ⚔ ♿

Saint Nicholas' Church   NORTH NEWBALD

St Nicholas' Church, North Newbald
t: (01430) 801068

open: Please contact keyholder for access, details
                   on the noticeboard.

description: A magnificent Norman church, the finest in the
                   East Riding. An aisle-less cruciform building
                   with a chancel of the late 14th-15th century.
                   Three Norman doorways.

facilities: 🐕 🎪 ♿

Saint Andrew's Church   PAULL

St Andrew's Church, Thorngumbald Road, Paull
t: (01482) 897693   **w:** standrewpaull.org.uk

open: Apr-Oct, Sat-Sun 1400-1600.

description: The church is in a beautiful setting overlooking
                   the Humber estuary. It was built soon after
                   1355 to replace a church in the village which
                   was broken down and inundated.

facilities: 🐕 ♿

Madhyamaka Buddhist Centre

POCKLINGTON

Madhyamaka Buddhist Centre, Kilnwick Percy Hall, Pocklington, YO42 1UF   **t:** (01759) 304832
w: madhyamaka.org

open: Parkland: daily. Main building: daily 1400-1700.

description: Madhyamaka Centre is a thriving Buddhist meditation centre founded in 1979. Situated just outside the town of Pocklington, near York.

facilities: ♨ ⚿ ⛉ ♿

Saint Ethelburga's Church

POCKLINGTON

St Ethelburga's Church, Great Givendale, Pocklington, YO42 1TT   **t:** (01759) 368123
w: allsaintspocklington.org.uk

open: All year, Fri-Sun 0900-1700.

description: A small church hidden away in a superb setting amongst trees at the head of a valley. A delight to all who discover it.

facilities: ⚿

Church of St Mary

SWINE

The Church of St Mary the Virgin, Swine, Main Street, Swine, HU11 4JE   **t:** (01964) 562259

open: Please contact keyholder for access, details on the noticeboard.

description: A Cistercian nunnery was founded at Swine in the mid-12th century and the medieval church was cruciform with central tower and transepts. Tower, nave and choir of late-12thC parish church remain. Collection of fine furnishings

facilities:

Church of St Mary the Virgin

WANSFORD

The Church of St Mary the Virgin, Nafferton Road, Wansford, YO25 8NT   **t:** (01377) 254372

open: All year, Sat-Sun 1000-1600.

description: Built 1866-8 for Tatton Sykes II by Street following the rejection of Pearson's 1865 design. Inside, a sumptuous Italian Gothic screen of marble, alabaster and iron, a richly-painted roof and a fine series of windows.

facilities:

1066 Battle Abbey and Battlefield

1066 Battle Abbey and Battlefield, High Street, Battle, TN33 0AD   **t:** (01424) 773792   **w:** english-heritage.org.uk

Open:	Apr-Sep, daily 1000-1800. Oct-Mar, daily 1000-1600.
Admission:	£6.30
Description:	An abbey founded by William the Conqueror on the site of the Battle of Hastings. The church altar is on the spot where King Harold was killed.
Facilities:	🍵 🐕 🛏 ♿

Preston Park, St. Peter's Church

Preston Park, St Peter's Church, Preston Road, Brighton, BN1 6SD
t: (020) 7213 0660
w: visitchurches.org.uk

Open:	Daily 1000-1600.
Description:	Rare example of an estate church within a town, retaining its original 13thC outward appearance. Inside, decorations from the Middle Ages and the Victorian era include substantial 14thC wall paintings .
Facilities:	🐕

Chiddingly Parish Church

CHIDDINGLY

Chiddingly Parish Church, Chiddingly, BN8 6HE
t: (01825) 872237   **w:** chiddingly.gov.uk/church

open: Daily, dawn-dusk.

description: Grade I Listed building with a ring of eight bells, the Jefferay Monument, Pelham buckles, traces of two Mass Dials, restored wooden graveboard and a Harmer terracotta.

facilities: ⚲ ⛩ ♿

Hove, St. Andrew

HOVE

Hove, St Andrew, Waterloo Street, Hove, BN3 1AQ
t: (020) 7213 0660   **w:** visitchurches.org.uk

open: All year, Sun 1200-1600.

description: This extended Italian Renaissance-style Regency church, by Sir Charles Barry, now contains high-quality 20thC fittings designed to create 'a little bit of Italy in Waterloo Street', while the chancel has a striking painted ceiling.

facilities: ⚲

aint Peters-on-the-Wall

aint Peters-on-the-Wall, East End Road, Bradwell-on-Sea,
M0 7PX   **t:** (01621) 776203   **w:** bradwellchapel.org

en: Daily.

scription: A 7thC Saxon chapel which is always open
                 and offers a small exhibition about its history,
                 and a bookstall. Evening services every
                 Sunday at 1800 during July and August.

cilities: 🐕 ♿

athedral Church of
t Mary and St Helen

athedral Church of St Mary and St Helen, Ingrave Road,
entwood, CM15 8AT   **t:** (01277) 265235
brentwood-cathedral.co.uk

en: Daily 1000-1700.

scription: Begun in 1989,
                 the current
                 cathedral was
                 designed by
                 leading Classical
                 architect Quinlan

                 Terry and was formally dedicated by Cardinal
                 Basil Hume in 1991.

cilities: 🍴 ♿

Chelmsford Cathedral

Chelmsford Cathedral, Cathedral Office, 53 New Street,
Chelmsford, CM1 1TY   t: (01245) 294480
w: chelmsfordcathedral.org.uk

open: Daily 0800-1800.

description: A late-medieval church, reordered in 1983 and
                   blending old with new. It became a cathedral
                   in 1914 when the Diocese of Chelmsford was
                   created. Modern sculpture and tapestry.

facilities: ⚔ ♿

Saint Botolphs Priory

Saint Botolphs Priory, Colchester
t: (01206) 282931

open: All year, daily.

description: The remains of a 12thC priory near the town
                   centre with a nave which has an impressive
                   arcaded west end. One of the first Augustinian
                   priories in England.

facilities: ⚔ ♿

Saint Michael and All Angels Church

Saint Michael and All Angels Church, Church Road, Copford Green, Colchester, CO6 1DA   **t:** (01206) 210488
w: copfordchurch.org.uk

open: All year, 0900-dusk.

description: A 12thC church in Romanesque style, with 12thC wall paintings.

facilities:

Saint Andrews Church, Greensted

St Andrew's Church, Greensted, Church Lane, Greensted Road, Greensted, CM5 9LA   **t:** (01992) 524005

open: All year, daily

description: The oldest wooden church in the world and the oldest wooden (stave-built) building in Europe.

facilities:

Saint James the Less Church

St James the Less Church, Church Lane, Little Tey, CO6 1HX
(01206) 211481

Open:	All year.
Description:	A 12thC church with 13th and 14thC wall paintings which have been uncovered and conserved without any restoration - virtually untouched since their original creation.
Facilities:	🐕 🪑 ♿

Rural Discovery Church

Rural Discovery Church, Saint Lawrence Hill, Saint Lawrence, Southminster, CM0 7LN   t: (01621) 779319

Open:	May-Sep, Sat-Sun, Bank Hols 1430-1630.
Admission:	£1.00
Description:	An active church, sited on hill overlooking River Blackwater. Exhibitions of local interest.
Facilities:	🍵 🐕 🪑 ♿

Waltham Abbey Church

Waltham Abbey Church, Highbridge Street, Waltham Abbey,
EN9 1DG   **t:** (01992) 767897
w: walthamabbeychurch.co.uk

open: Apr-Sep 1000-1800. Oct-Mar 1000-1600.

description: A Norman church, the reputed
site of King Harold's tomb. There is a lady
chapel with a crypt which houses a visitors'
centre and shop.

facilities: ▭ 🕴 🛆 ♿

Willingale Churches

Willingale Churches, The Street, Willingale, CM5 0SH
t: (01992) 652295

open: Daily, dawn-dusk.

description: Two ancient churches in one churchyard, side
by side. On this site since Norman times. A
village setting on the Essex Way.

facilities: 🐕 🛆 ♿

hurch of
aint John Baptist

hurch of Saint John Baptist, Market Place, Cirencester,
_7 2BQ   **t:** (01285) 659317   **w:** cirenparish.co.uk

en: Apr-Oct, daily 1000-1700. Nov-Mar, daily
                1000-1600.

scription: One of the wool churches of the Cotswolds
                with 15thC pulpit, tower, three-storey fan-
                vaulted porch and Anne Boleyn cup.

cilities: 🍽 🏃 ♿

dda's Chapel
English Heritage)

dda's Chapel (English Heritage), Deerhurst
(01684) 295027   **w:** english-heritage.org.uk

en: Apr-Oct, daily 1000-1800. Nov-Mar, daily
                1000-1600.

scription: Rare Saxon chapel dating
                back to 1056, attached to a
                half-timbered farmhouse. It lay
                undiscovered for many years
                and has been partly rebuilt and
                restored.

cilities: 🏃 ♿

Saint Mary Virgin Fairford

FAIRFOR

St Mary the Virgin, High Street, Fairford, GL7 4AF
t: (01285) 712611

open: Summer: daily 1000-1700. Winter: daily 1000
1600.

description: A late-15thC,
Perpendicular-style
church with a set of 28
stained glass, medieval
windows. The graveyard
contains some fine
examples of Cotswold
tombs including several that have Listed
Building status.

facilities: 🐕 ⛱ ♿

Gloucester Cathedral

GLOUCESTE

Gloucester Cathedral, Westgate Street, Gloucester,
GL1 2LR   **t:** (01452) 528095
w: gloucestercathedral.org.uk

open: All year, Mon-Fri 0730-1815, Sat 0730-1715,
Sun 0730-1600.
admission: £3.00

description: An architectura
gem made of honey-
coloured limestone with
crypt, cloisters and Chapter
House set in its precincts.

facilities: 🖥 🕺 ⛱ ♿

Saint Mary's Church

KEMPLEY

St Mary's Church, Kempley
t: (01531) 822468   **w:** english-heritage.org.uk

open: Apr-Oct, Mon-Sun 1000-1800.

description: A delightful Norman church with superb wall
                paintings from the 12th-14th centuries which
                were only discovered beneath whitewash in
                1871.

facilities:

Parish Church of St Mary

PAINSWICK

Parish Church of St Mary, Painswick, GL6 6UT
t: (01452) 814795   **w:** gloucestershire.gov.uk

open: See website for details.

description: Fourteenth-century church gradually extended
                in later centuries. The tower houses 14 bells,
                the earliest of which dates from 1686.

facilities:

Saint Mary The Virgin with St Mary Magdalene Church

TETBURY

St Mary The Virgin with St Mary Magdalene Church, Church Street, Tetbury, GL8 8DN   **t:** (01666) 502333

open:	Daily 0900-1700.
description:	Built in 1781 in Georgian Gothic style. The spire is the fourth highest in England, measuring 186ft, and is part of the old medieval church. Recently restored.
facilities:	

Old Baptist Chapel and Court

TEWKESBURY

Old Baptist Chapel and Court, Church Street, Tewkesbury, GL20 5RZ   **t:** (01684) 299893   **w:** gloucestershire.gov.uk

open:	All year, daily.
description:	Constructed in the 15th century as a three-bay house and later adapted as a chapel for worship. Modernised in 1720 and restored 1976-1979.
facilities:	

Tewkesbury Abbey

TEWKESBURY

Tewkesbury Abbey, Church Street, Tewkesbury, GL20 5RZ
t: (01684) 850959   **w:** tewkesburyabbey.org.uk

open: All year, daily 0800-1800.

description: Superb Norman abbey with 14thC vaulting and windows. Largest surviving Norman tower in the country. Formerly a Benedictine monastery, it is larger than many cathedrals.

facilities: ⬛ ✕ 🎋 ♿

Hailes Abbey

WINCHCOMBE

Hailes Abbey, Winchcombe, GL54 5PB
t: (01242) 602398   **w:** english-heritage.org.uk/hailes

open: Apr-June, daily 1000-1700. July-Aug, daily 1000-1800. Sep, daily 1000-1700. Oct, daily 1000-1600.

admission: £3.30

description: Standing in secluded Cotswold pastureland are the remains of this 13thC Cistercian abbey, built by Richard, Earl of Cornwall.

facilities: ⬛ ✕ 🎋 ♿

Bolton Parish Church

BOLTON

Bolton Parish Church, St Peters Bolton-Le-Moors,
Churchgate, Bolton, BL1 1PS   **t:** (01204) 533847
w: boltonparishchurch.co.uk

open: Apr-Sep, Tue-Sat 1000-1500. Oct-Mar, Tue-
                   Sat 1000-1400.

description: Built in 1871, this Victorian Gothic-style
                   church is said to have the tallest parish church
                   tower in Lancashire. The museum corner has
                   stone from the previous Saxon and Norman
                   buildings.

facilities: 🐕 ♿

Manchester Cathedral

MANCHESTER

Manchester Cathedral, Cathedral Yard, Manchester, M3 1SX
t: (0161) 833 2220

open: All year, Mon-Fri 0900-1730, Sat 0900-1530,
                   Sun 0900-1830, Bank Hols 0900-1630.

description: Dedicated to St
Mary, St Denys and St George,
this 15thC Perpendicular church
became a collegiate church in
1421 and was raised to cathedral
status in 1847.

facilities: ☕ 🐕 ♿

Saint Ann's Church

St Ann's Church, St Ann's Street, Manchester, M2 7LF
t: (0161) 834 0239   w: st-ann.org.uk

open: All year, Mon-Sat 0945-1645.

description: This 18thC church
                   contains a painting
                   from the School of
                   Caracci, stained glass
                   by W Peckitt of York,
                   and is the third oldest
                   building in Manchester
                   city centre.

facilities:

Chadkirk Chapel

Chadkirk Chapel, Vale Road, Romiley, Stockport,
SK6 3LD   t: (0161) 430 5611
w: chadkirkchapel.org.uk

open: Apr-Sep, Sat-Sun 1300-1700, Oct-Mar, Sat-
                   Sun 1200-1600.

description: Beautifully restored 14thC chapel set in
                   the heart of Chadkirk country estate in the
                   picturesque Goyt valley. Relax and cherish the
                   peace and tranquillity inside the chapel.

facilities:

Abbey of Our Lady and Saint John

BEECH

Abbey of Our Lady and Saint John, Beech, GU34 4AP
t: (01420) 562145

open: Daily.

description: Alton Abbey is home for a community of Benedictine monks. The abbey church and conventual buildings, built of local flint, are to a design by Sir Charles Nicholson.

facilities: 🍴🐕♿

Beaulieu Abbey

BROCKENHURST

Beaulieu Abbey, Brockenhurst, SO42 7XN
t: (01590) 612345   **w:** beaulieuabbey.co.uk

open: May-Sep, 1000-1800, Oct-May 1000-1700.

description: Former Cistercian monastery founded in 1204. Although a great deal was destroyed during the reign of Henry VIII, there is still much to see, including an exhibition of monastic life.

facilities: 🐕♿

Saint Nicholas Church

BROCKENHURST

St Nicholas Church, Church Lane, Brockenhurst, SO42 7UB
t: (01590) 624584   **w:** brockenhurstchurch.com

open: Apr-Sep, Mon-Sat 1430-1700.

description: Norman church, oldest in the New Forest, mentioned in the Domesday Book. Grave of Brusher Mills. New Zealand war graves of World War I.

facilities:

All Saints East Meon

EAST MEON

All Saints, East Meon
t: (01730) 823221
w: eastmeon.net/allsaints/homeoriginal.htm

open: Daily 0830-dusk.

description: A fine cross-shaped Norman church with a square central spire and decoration similar to Winchester Cathedral. Look out for the black marble Tournai font which dates from around 1150.

facilities:

Saint Andrew's Church

HAMBLE

St Andrew's Church, High Street,
Hamble, SO31 4JF
t: (023) 8045 2148
w: st-andrew-hamble.org

open: All year, Thu 0930-1200, Sat-Sun 0930-1200.

description: Built over 900 years ago, the church contains
fine examples of Norman architecture plus
two modern tapestries made by the people of
Hamble. New, modern, stained glass window.

facilities: 🐕 ⛱ ♿

Sandham Memorial Chapel

NR NEWBURY

Sandham Memorial Chapel, Harts Lane, Burghclere, Nr
Newbury, RG20 9JT   **t:** (01635) 278394
w: nationaltrust.org.uk/sandham

open: Mar, Sat-Sun 1100-1600. Apr-Oct, Wed-Sun
1100-1700. Nov, Sat-Sun 1100-1600. Dec,
Sat-Sun 1100-1500.

admission: £3.50

description: A 1920s chapel built for Stanley Spencer to
fill with murals inspired by his World War I
experiences.

facilities: 🐕 ⛱ ♿

Saint Peters Church

St Peters Church, Church Path, The Square, Petersfield,
GU32 3HS   t: (01730) 260213   w: stpetersfield.org.uk

open: Daily 0900-1700.

description: St Peter's was described by Pevsner as 'one
of the most interesting Norman churches
in Hampshire'. Remodelling in 1999 further
enhanced this Grade I Listed building.

facilities: 🐾 ♿

Catholic Cathedral of St John

Catholic Cathedral of St John, Edinburgh Road, Portsmouth,
PO1 3HG   t: (023) 9282 6170
w: portsmouthcatholiccathedral.org.uk

open: Daily 0800-1730.

description: A Victorian church with
wooden vaulted ceiling.
Restored in 2002. Awarded
'Best Restored Building in
Portsmouth'. The Cathedral
Discovery Centre offers a large
range of books and religious
items.

facilities: 💻 🐾 ♿

Portsmouth Cathedral

PORTSMOUTH

Portsmouth Cathedral, High Street, Portsmouth, PO1 2HH
t: (023) 9282 3300   w: portsmouthcathedral.org.uk

open:	Daily 0700-1900.
description:	Maritime cathedral with strong seafaring links. Tomb of unknown sailor from the Mary Rose. D-Day memorial window. The final stages of building were completed in 1991.
facilities:	

Saint Mary's Church

PORTSMOUTH

Saint Mary's Church, Fratton Road, Portsmouth, PO1 5PA
t: (023) 9282 2687   w: portseaparish.co.uk

open:	Daily 0900-1200.
description:	St Mary's has been described as the finest Victorian building in Hampshire. Designed just over 100 years ago by Arthur Blomfield. Finest Walker organ in England.
facilities:	

Romsey Abbey

ROMSEY

Romsey Abbey, Church Lane, Romsey, SO51 8EP
: (01794) 513125   **w:** romseyabbey.org.uk

open: Daily 0830-1730.

description: Fine Norman and Early-English abbey, Saxon
                foundations and roods.
                Tomb of Earl Mountbatten
                of Burma. Broadlands
                pew. Active parish church
                with fine choral tradition.

facilities: ⚲ ⛱ ♿

Netley Abbey

SOUTHAMPTON

Netley Abbey, 1 Abbey Hill, Netley, Southampton, SO31 5FB
: (023) 9258 1059   **w:** english-heritage.org.uk

open: Apr-Sep 1000-1800. Oct-Mar 1000-1500.

description: The most complete
surviving Cistercian monastery in
southern England, dating from the 13th
century. Converted into a Tudor mansion
after the Dissolution.

facilities: 🐕 ⛱ ♿

Titchfield Abbey

Titchfield Abbey, Mill Lane, Titchfield, PO15 5RA
t: (01424) 775705   **w:** english-heritage.org.uk

open:	Apr-Sep, daily 1000-1700. Oct-Mar, daily 1000-1600.
description:	The remains of a 13thC abbey overshadowed by a grand Tudor gatehouse.
facilities:	🐕 ♿

Hospital of St Cross & Almshouse of Noble Poverty

Hospital of St Cross & Almshouse of Noble Poverty, The Hospital of St Cross, St Cross Road, Winchester, SO23 9SD
t: (01962) 851375   **w:** stcrosshospital.co.uk

open:	Apr-Oct, Mon-Sat 0930-1700, Sun 1300-1700 Nov-Mar, Mon-Sat 1030-1530.
admission:	£2.50

description: In a serene and picturesque setting by the Water Meadows, the Hospital of St Cross is a beautiful group of Grade I Listed buildings dating from 1132.

facilities:	🤸 ♿

Winchester Cathedral

WINCHESTER

Winchester Cathedral, The Close, Winchester, SO23 9LS
: (01962) 857225   **w**: winchester-cathedral.org.uk

open: All year, Mon-Sat 0830-1800, Sun 0830-1730.
admission: £4.00

description: Magnificent medieval
cathedral, soaring Gothic nave
converted from Norman 12thC
illuminated Winchester Bible,
Jane Austen's tomb, library,
gallery, crypt, chapels.

facilities: 💻 🚭 🍽 ♿

All Saints

BROCKHAMPTON

All Saints (Thatched), Brockhampton, HR1 4SD
: (01432) 860365   **w**: brockhampton.com/church.htm

open: All year.

description: Designed by architect William Lethaby and
completed in 1902, this Grade I listed building
is a superb monument to the Arts and Crafts
movement. Don't miss the Burne-Jones
tapestries.

facilities: 🐕 ♿

Hereford Cathedral

HEREFORD

Hereford Cathedral, Cathedral Office, The Cloisters, Cathedral Close, Hereford, HR1 2NG **t:** (01432) 374202
w: herefordcathedral.org

open: Daily 0730-1730.

description: Built on a 7thC church site. Mixture of styles from Norman to Early English, decorated to Perpendicular.

facilities:

Mappa Mundi & Chained Library Exhibition

HEREFORD

Mappa Mundi & Chained Library Exhibition, Hereford Cathedral, 5 The Cloisters, Hereford, HR1 2NG
t: (01432) 374202 **w:** herefordcathedral.co.uk

open: Apr-Sep, Mon-Sat 1000-1630, Sun 1100-1530. Oct-Mar, Mon-Sat 1000-1630.

admission: £4.50

description: The new library of Hereford Cathedral is home to the unique Mappa Mundi, the largest and most complete map in the world, drawn in 1289.

facilities:

See pages 2-3 for key to symbols

Rotherwas Chapel

Rotherwas Chapel, Chapel Road, Hereford
t: (0121) 625 6820   **w:** english-heritage.org.uk

open: All year, please contact keyholder on 07795 120586.

description: A small Roman Catholic chapel originally of 14thC but rebuilt in 16thC with unbuttressed west tower of a later date with an interesting mid-Victorian side chapel.

facilities:

Saint John Medieval Museum

Saint John Medieval Museum, Coningsby Hospital, Widemarsh Street, Hereford, HR4 9HN
t: (01432) 274903

open: All year, Wed,Sat 1100-1500.
admission: £2.00

description: Small museum and chapel dating back to the 13th century. Contains armour and relics relating to the Order of St John.

facilities:

KILPECK

Kilpeck Church
(Church of St David and St Mary)

Kilpeck Church (Church of St David and St Mary), Kilpeck,
HR2 9DN   t: (01981) 570315

open: All year.

description: Norman Romanesque church built in 1140
                  and standing almost unchanged. Famed
                  worldwide for its carvings, both inside and
                  outside. Situated in a medieval village.

facilities: 🐕 🪑 ♿

MADLEY

Madley Church

Madley Church, Madley, HR2 9LP
t: (01981) 250557   w: madley-peterchurch-parishes.org

open: Daily 0900-1700.

description: Madley parish church dates entirely between
                  1050 and 1350. A place of pilgrimage in
                  medieval times, this large and fascinating
                  church should not be missed today.

facilities: 🐕 ♿

Saint Mary the Virgin

St Mary the Virgin, Little Hormead, Buntingford, SG9 0LS
: (020) 7213 0660   **w:** visitchurches.org.uk

open: Daily 1000-1600.

description: In a peaceful rural setting, St Mary's is an unaltered example of a simple two-celled Norman church. The remarkable 12thC north

door, with its original decorative ironwork, is now preserved inside the church.

facilities:

Cathedral and Abbey Church of St Alban

Cathedral and Abbey Church of St Alban,
The Chapter House, St Albans, AL1 1BY
: (01727) 860780   **w:** stalbanscathedral.org.uk

open: Daily 0800-1745.

description: A Norman abbey church on the site of the martyrdom of St Alban, Britain's first Christian martyr. The 13thC shrine has been restored and is a centre of ecumenical worship.

facilities:

Stanstead Abbots Saint James' Church

STANSTEAD ABBOTS

Stanstead Abbots St James' Church, Roydon Road, Stanstead Abbots, SG12 8JU   **t:** (020) 7213 0660
w: visitchurches.org.uk

open: Jun-Sep, Sun 1430-1700.

description: The simple exterior conceals one of the best ecclesiastical interiors in Hertfordshire. Monuments include a fine Elizabethan tomb to Sir Edward Baeshe, civil servant to four monarchs, and builder of the north chapel.

facilities: 🐕

All Saints Margaret Street

LONDON

All Saints Margaret Street, 7 Margaret Street, London, W1W 8JG   **t:** (020) 7636 1788
w: allsaintsmargaretstreet.org.uk

open: Daily 0700-1900.

description: This church is the most influential of all the buildings of its architect, William Butterfield, being the first example of the constructional use of coloured materials.

facilities: 🐕 ⏻ ♿

All Souls Church, Langham Place

LONDON

All Souls Church, Langham Place, 2 All Souls Place, London, W1B 3DA **t:** (020) 7580 3522 **w:** allsouls.org

open: All year, Mon-Fri 0930-1800, Sun 0800-2000.

description: Designed by John Nash and built in 1824 as the pivot point of his plan for Regent Street. Painting on east wall, 'Behold The Man' by Westall, was presented by George IV.

facilities:

Bevis Marks Synagogue

LONDON

Bevis Marks Synagogue, Bevis Marks, London, EC3A 5DQ
t: (020) 7626 1274 **w:** bevismarks.org.uk

open: All year, Mon-Fri 1100-1300, Sun 1030-1230.
admission: £3.00

description: Completed in 1701, this is the oldest synagogue still in use in Britain. The interior has changed very little since it was built. Look out for the beautiful Rennaissance-style ark.

facilities:

Central Hall Westminster

Central Hall Westminster, Storey's Gate, London, SW1H 9NH
t: (020) 7222 8010   w: c-h-w.com

Open: All year, Mon-Fri 0800-1800, Sat-Sun 0900-1800.

Description: Take a guided tour at this unique, historic Edwardian building, see the Great Hall with its magnificent organ and the superb view from the balcony.

Facilities: 🖥 🏃 ♿

Chapel Royal of St Peter Ad Vincula

Chapel Royal of St Peter Ad Vincula, Tower of London, London, EC3N 4AB   t: (020) 7488 5689   w: hrp.org.uk

Open: All year, Sun 0915-1200.

Description: The Tudor burial place of Queen Anne Boleyn, Queen Catherine Howard and Sir Thomas More.

Facilities: 🖥 🏃 🛏 ♿

Church of St Anne's Limehouse

LONDON

Church of St Anne's Limehouse, Commercial Road, London, E14 7HP **t:** (020) 7987 1502

open: All year, Sun 1000-1300.

description: A 1730 Hawksmoor masterpiece, with the exterior fully restored. On display is the Gray and Davison organ which won the gold medal at the Great Exhibition of 1851.

facilities: 🐕 ⛱ ♿

Guards Chapel

LONDON

Guards Chapel, Wellington Barracks, Birdcage Walk, London, SW1E 6HQ **t:** (020) 7414 3228

open: All year, Mon-Thu 1000-1600, Fri 1000-1400, Sun 1100-1230.

description: Household Division Regimental Chapels built in 1838, bombed in 1944 and rebuilt in 1963. There are displays of memorial books, colours and standards.

facilities: 🐕 ⛱ ♿

Hindu Temple
(Shri Swaminarayan Mandir)

Hindu Temple (Shri Swaminarayan Mandir), 105/115
Brentfield Road, Neasden, London, NW10 8JP
t: (020) 8965 2651   w: mandir.org

open: Daily 0900-1800.

description: The first traditional Hindu Mandir in Europe,
                 carved and constructed entirely according to
                 the ancient Shipsashtras (treatise on temple
                 architecture). Also Hinduism exhibition.

facilities: 💻 🏃 ♿

Southwark Cathedral

Southwark Cathedral, London Bridge, London,
SE1 9DA   t: (020) 7367 6700 & (020) 7367 6734
w: southwark.anglican.org/cathedral

open: All year, Mon-Fri 0800-1800, Sat, Sun, Bank
                 Hols 0900-1800.
admission: £4.00

description: London's oldest Gothic church
building with links to William Shakespeare and
US-university benefactor John Harvard. The
churchyard gardens contain a memorial to
Mahomet Weyonomon of the Mohegan tribe.

facilities: 💻 🏃 🪑 ♿

Saint Alfege's Church

St Alfege's Church, Greenwich Church Street, London,
SE10 9BJ   **w:** st-alfege.org

open: All year, Sat 1130-1600, Sun 1200-1600. Other times by appointment.

description: Hawksmoor Church where Henry VIII was baptised. Thomas Tallis and General Wolfe are buried in the vaults. Site of martyrdom of St Alfege, Archbishop of Canterbury, in 1012.

facilities: 🐕 ♿

Saint Brides Fleet Street

St Brides Fleet Street, Fleet Street, London,
EC4Y 8AU   **t:** (020) 7427 0133

open: Please phone for details.

description: This church, restored by Sir Christopher Wren, has a crypt museum which tells the story of the six previous churches that stood here. Also, display of local printing industry.

facilities: 🐕 ♿

Saint Clement Danes Church

St Clement Danes Church, Strand, London, WC2R 1DH
(020) 7242 8282

Open: Daily 0900-1600.

Description: This is the 'Oranges and Lemons'
                  church, and features include a
                  Grinling Gibbons pulpit and Samuel
                  Johnson statue. Central church
                  of Royal Air Force with Books of
                  Remembrance.

Facilities: 🏃 ♿

Saint George's Church Hanover Square

St George's Church Hanover Square, St George Street,
London, W1S 1FX   **t:** (020) 7629 0874
: stgeorgeshanoversquare.org

Open: All year, Mon-Fri 0800-1600, Sun 0800-1200.

Description: Classical church building designed by John
                  James and consecrated in 1725. Early-16thC
                  Flemish stained glass from Antwerp. 'Last
                  Supper' painted by William Kent.

Facilities: 🏃 ♿

Saint Giles Church Cripplegate

St Giles Church Cripplegate, Fore Street, London, EC2Y 8D/
t: (020) 7638 1997   **w:** stgilescripplegate.com

open: All year, Mon-Fri 1100-1600, Sun 0800-1630.

description: A church of great historical and architectural interest. Roman wall in churchyard. John Milton is buried here, and Oliver Cromwell married here. Recitals held.

facilities:

Saint Giles-in-the-Fields Church

St Giles-in-the-Fields Church, St Giles High Street, London, WC2H 8LG   **t:** (020) 7240 2532   **w:** stgilesonline.org

open: All year, Mon-Fri 0930-1600.

description: Built 1731-1733 and designed by the architect Flitcroft, the church contains parish records from 1615. The plague started in the parish. Also famous for the St Giles Bowl.

facilities:

Saint James's Church
Piccadilly

St James's Church Piccadilly, 197 Piccadilly, London,
W1J 9LL   **t:** (020) 7734 4511   **w:** st-james-piccadilly.org

Open: Daily 0800-1830.

Description: The church, designed
by Sir Christopher Wren,
opened in 1684. Regular
concerts, services
and lectures. Market
Wednesday to Saturday.
Antiques market on
Tuesday.

Facilities: 💻 🏋 🏓 ♿

Saint John's Church

St John's Church, Hyde Park Crescent, London, W2 2QD
t: (020) 7262 1732   **w:** stjohns-hydepark.com

Open: All year, Mon-Fri 0900-1730.

Description: An early Gothic Revival building, built in 1832
and noted for its excellent modern glass and
altar.

Facilities: 🐕 ♿

Saint Margaret's Church

LONDON

St Margaret's Church, Parliament Square, London, SW1P 3JX
t: (020) 7654 4840   **w:** westminster-abbey.org

open: All year, Mon-Fri 0930-1545, Sat 0930-1345,
                Sun 1400-1700.

description: A fine 16thC building with notable medieval
                and modern stained glass. The burial place
                of Sir Walter Raleigh and parish church of the
                House of Commons.

facilities:

Saint Martin-in-the-Fields Church

LONDON

St Martin-in-the-Fields Church, Trafalgar Square, London,
WC2N 4JJ   **t:** (020) 7766 1100   **w:** smitf.org

open: From Oct, daily 0900-1800.

description: One of London's best-loved churches, with
                a superb arts venue, holding more than 350
                concerts every year. The18thC crypt houses a
                cafe, a shop and the London Brass Rubbing
                Centre.

facilities:

Saint Mary Le Bow Church

LONDON

St Mary Le Bow Church, Cheapside, London, EC2V 6AU
t: (020) 7248 5139   **w:** stmarylebow.co.uk

open: All year, Mon 0815-1745, Tue 0730-1745, Wed 0815-1745, Thu 0815-1805, Fri 0815-1305.

description: Rebuilt by Christopher Wren after the Great Fire of London. Home to the Bow Bells. The Norman crypt with its chapel is the oldest parochial building still in use in London.

facilities: ▄ ⚒ ♿

Saint Olave's Church Hart Street

LONDON

St Olave's Church Hart Street, 8 Hart Street, London, EC3R 7NB   **t:** (020) 7488 4318   **w:** sanctuaryinthecity.co.uk

open: Daily 0830-1700.

description: Church dating from 1056 and the burial place of Samuel Pepys. This is the parish church of Trinity House with many interesting historical features. Has strong Norwegian links.

facilities: ⚒ ♿

Saint Paul's Cathedral

LONDON

St Paul's Cathedral, St Paul's Churchyard, London,
EC4M 8AD   **t:** (020) 7246 8357   **w:** stpauls.co.uk

open: All year, Mon-Sat 0830-1600.
admission: £9.50

 description: The cathedral was designed by Sir
Christopher Wren and was built between 1675 and
1710 after its predecessor was destroyed in the
Great Fire of London.

facilities: ☕ 🚻 ♿

Saint Peter's Church

LONDON

St Peter's Church, 119 Eaton Square, London, SW1W 9AL
t: (020) 7235 4482   **w:** stpetereatonsquare.co.uk

open: All year, Mon-Tue, Thu-Fri 0730-1700, Wed
0730-1300.

description: Church built by Hakewill in 1827 and enlarged
by Blomfield in 1875. It is the scene of many
fashionable weddings. Rebuilt and opened in
1992 following a fire in 1987.

facilities: 🚻 ♿

Westminster Abbey

LONDON

Westminster Abbey, Parliament Square, London, SW1P 3PA
t: (020) 7222 5152   w: westminster-abbey.org

open:	See website for details.
admission:	£10.00

description: One of Britain's finest Gothic buildings. Scene of the coronation, marriage and burial of British monarchs. Nave and cloisters, royal chapels and Undercroft Museum.

facilities: 🖥 🚶 ♿

Westminster Cathedral

LONDON

Westminster Cathedral, Victoria Street, London, SW1P 1QW
t: (020) 7798 9055   w: westminstercathedral.org.uk

open:	All year, Mon-Fri 0700-1900, Sat-Sun 0800-1900.
admission:	£6.00

description: England's principal Roman Catholic cathedral completed in 1903. Brick built in Byzantine style with interior marbles, mosaics and famous 'Stations of the Cross' by Eric Gill.

facilities: 🚶 ♿

Saint George's Church

ARRETON

Saint George's Church, Arreton, PO30 3AA
t: (01983) 865357   w: st-george-arreton.org.uk

open: Daily.

description: A 12thC church in old village centre near
                   manor and inn. Saxon doorway, some fine
                   marble memorials. Burma Star memorial
                   window.

facilities: 🐕 🁢 ♿

Saint Mildred's Church
and Church Centre

EAST COWES

Saint Mildred's Church and Church Centre, Beatrice Avenue,
Whippingham, East Cowes, PO32 6LW
t: (01983) 200107   w: iowight.com/stmildreds

open: May-Oct, Mon-Fri 1000-1600.

description: Church designed by Prince Albert, a place
                   of worship when Queen Victoria stayed at
                   Osborne House. Church and centre with
                   displays of royal and local photographs and
                   artefacts.

facilities: ☕ 🐕 🁢 ♿

Saint Agnes

FRESHWATER

t Agnes (Thatched), Gate Lane, Freshwater Bay, Freshwater, O40 9PY   **t:** (01983) 755589

pen: All year.

escription: This pretty church is the only thatched church on the Isle of Wight. It was built on land donated by the son of poet laureate Alfred Lord Tennyson in 1908.

cilities: 🐕 ♿

riars

AYLESFORD

e Friars, Aylesford Priory, Aylesford, ME20 7BX (01622) 717272   **w:** thefriars.org.uk

pen: Apr-Sep, daily 1000-1700. Oct-Mar, daily 1000-1600.

escription: A 13thC priory with 14thC cloisters and a shrine. Visitors can see sculpture and ceramics by  contemporary artists. Medieval barns, pottery, upholstery workshops can be seen.

cilities: ☕ 🏃 🪑 ♿

Canterbury Cathedral

CANTERBUR

Canterbury Cathedral, The Precincts, Canterbury, CT1 2EH
t: (01227) 762862 **w:** canterbury-cathedral.org

open: All year, Mon-Sat 0900-1700, Sun 1230-1400
admission: £5.50

description: Founded in AD597, it is the Mother Church of Anglican Communion and has a Romanesque crypt, 12thC Gothic quire and 14thC nave. Site of Thomas Becket's murder in AD1170.

facilities: 🍴 🐕 ⛱ ♿

Saint Augustine's Abbey

CANTERBUR

St Augustine's Abbey, Longport, Canterbury, CT1 1TF
t: (01227) 767345 **w:** english-heritage.org.uk

open: Apr-Jun, Wed-Sun 1000-1700. Jul-Aug, daily 1000-1800. Sep-Mar, Sun 1100-1700.
admission: £4.00

description: Now a World Heritage Site, this Benedictine Abbey was founded in AD598 by St Augustine. The remains include a Norman church and ruins of the 7thC church of St Pancras.

facilities: 🚶 ⛱ ♿

Church of
St Mary Magdalene

Church of St Mary Magdalene, Cobham, DA12 3DH
(01474) 814524   **w:** cobham-luddesdowne.org

Open: Daily 0900-1600.

Description: An historic medieval church housing a superb
                   collection of monumental brasses.

Facilities: 🐕 ♿

Cooling St James

Cooling St James, Main Road, Cooling, ME3 8DG
(020) 7213 0660   **w:** visitchurches.org.uk

Open: Daily 1000-1600.

Description: In a desolate position on Thames marshes and
                   believed to be the setting for the opening of
                   Dickens' Great Expectations. The interior is
                   impressively spacious, and the vestry is lined
                   with cockle shells.

Facilities: 🐕 ⛱ ♿

Saint Mary Charity

St Mary of Charity, Faversham
t: (01795) 532592

open:　　　　All year, daily 1000-1700.

description:　　The church was founded in the medieval
era, although the spire, which dominates
Faversham, is was built in the 18th century.
Look out for the rare medieval painted pillar.

facilities:　　　🐾 ♿

Fordwich St. Mary the Virgin

Fordwich St Mary the Virgin, The Drove, Fordwich, CT2 0DE
t: (020) 7213 0660　　**w:** visitchurches.org.uk

open:　　　　Please contact keyholder for access.

description: At the centre of
England's smallest town and
containing craftsmanship
spanning 900 years. Particularly
notable is the Fordwich Stone
from c1100, exquisitely carved as
a shrine for a saint's relics, possibly those of St Augustine.

facilities:　　　🐾

Bayham Abbey

Bayham Abbey, Lamberhurst, TN3 8DE
t: (01892) 890381   **w:** english-heritage.org.uk

open:	Apr-Sep, daily 1100-1700.
admission:	£3.60

description:	Impressive abbey ruins, founded in 1208 by Premonstratensian monks and dissolved by Wolsey in 1525. Ruins of church buildings and gatehouse, set in valley of River Teise.

facilities: ⚔ 🪑 ♿

Minster Abbey

Minster Abbey, Minster-in-Thanet, CT12 4HF
t: (01843) 821254

open:	Chapel: daily. Tours: Please phone for details.

description:	Founded in 670, the Abbey was destroyed in 840 and restored in 1027. Two wings of the old building with Norman crypt contain the ruin of a church tower.

facilities: 🐕 ♿

Saint Michael's Church

St Michael's Church, Old Church Lane, East Peckham,
Nr Tonbridge, TN12 5NF   **t:** (01622) 813687
w: stmichaelseastpeckham.co.uk

open: Apr-Oct, daily 1000-1600.

description: Originally Norman, the church has 14thC piers
and arches, windows and south porch which
are mainly 15th century and an attractive
weathervane dated 1704 on its shingled
spirelet.

facilities: 🐕 🛆 ♿

Rochester Cathedral

Rochester Cathedral, The Precinct,
Rochester, ME1 1SX
t: (01634) 401301
w: rochestercathedral.org

open: All year, Mon-Fri 0700-1800, Sat-Sun 0700-
1700.

admission: £4.00

description: Consecrated in AD604, the present building
dates from 1080. A blend of Norman and
Gothic architecture raised above a crypt with
medieval wall paintings.

facilities: 💺 🏃 ♿

Sandwich St Peter

Sandwich St Peter, High Street, Sandwich, CT13 9EQ
t: (020) 7213 0660   **w:** visitchurches.org.uk

open: Daily 1000-1600.

description: The present medieval
church of St Peter's was
constructed at a time of
great prosperity for the town
as one of the Cinque Ports,
and the tower dominates the
skyline. The building exhibits
high-quality craftsmanship.

facilities: 🐕

West Stourmouth, All Saints Church

West Stourmouth, All Saints Church, All Saints Church,
Stourmouth, CT3 1HT   **t:** (020) 7213 0660
w: visitchurches.org.uk

open: Daily 1000-1600.

description: The tall narrow walls typify All Saints' Saxon
origin. Considerably rebuilt after an earthquake
in 1382, and with massive brick buttresses to
counteract subsidence. Inside is a fascinating
mixture of furnishings of different ages.

facilities: 🐕 ♿

Saint Michaels Church

St Michael's Church, Bracewell, Barnoldswick, BB18 5EP
t: (01282) 812028   **w:** barnoldswick.parish.btinternet.co.uk

open: Please contact the keyholder in the Old Post Office or the Vicarage for details.

description: Dating from 1100, this was once the private chapel of the Tempest family. Contains pews from the workshop of Robert 'Mouseman' Thompson, look out for his mouse trademark.

facilities: ✕

Blackburn Cathedral

Blackburn Cathedral, Cathedral Offices, Cathedral Close, Blackburn, BB1 5AA   **t:** (01254) 51491
w: blackburn.anglican.org/cathedral

open: All year, Mon-Sat 0800-1700.

description: Blackburn Cathedral has a Georgian nave with 20thC extensions, featuring sculptures by John Hayward and Josephina De Vasconcellos, and Burne-Jones windows.

facilities: ✕ ♿

Whalley Abbey

CLITHEROE

Whalley Abbey, Whalley, Clitheroe, BB7 9SS
t: (01254) 828400   **w:** whalleyabbey.co.uk

open: Daily 1000-dusk.
admission: £2.00

description: Fourteenth-century Cistercian abbey ruins
                 set in beautiful countryside beside the River
                 Calder, with mini woodland trail, riverside path,
                 exhibition centre, gift shop and coffee shop.

facilities:

Lancaster Priory Church

LANCASTER

Lancaster Priory Church, Castle Hill,
Lancaster, LA1 1YZ
t: (01524) 65338
w: priory.lancaster.ac.uk

open: All year, daily 1000-1630.

description: This 15thC church stands on the site of
                 a priory founded in 1094 and contains
                 magnificent oak-canopied choir stalls. There
                 are also modern embroideries on display.

facilities:

Pilling Saint John the Baptist Old Church

Pilling, St John the Baptist Old Church, School Lane, Pilling, PR3 6AA   **t:** (020) 7213 0660   **w:** visitchurches.org.uk

open: Please contact keyholder for access.

description: Constructed in 1717, the interior is a survival of a perfect Georgian preaching box where the sermon was all-important in worship. In 1813 the walls were raised to accommodate galleries for the growing congregation.

facilities:

Whalley Parish Church

Whalley Parish Church, Church Lane, Whalley, BB7 9SY
t: (01254) 823249   **w:** whalleypc.com

open: Daily 1400-1600.

description: A 13thC church, with 15thC misericords and screens, 17thC brasses, 18thC organ, a chained book and three Saxon crosses.

facilities:

Church of Saint Mary the Virgin

Church of Saint Mary the Virgin, Rectory Lane, Bottesford, NG13 0DG   **t:** (01949) 843615

open: All year, Mon-Thu 0900-1430.

description: Saint Mary the Virgin, Bottesford, is a magnificent cruciform church with a tower and 210ft spire, in a beautiful setting by the river Devon.

facilities: ▆ ⚒ ⊓ ♿

Leicester Cathedral

Leicester Cathedral, 21 St Martin's, Leicester, LE1 5DE
t: (0116) 262 5294   **w:** cathedral.leicester.anglican.org

open: All year, Mon-Sat 0800-1800, Sun 0700-1700.

description: The Guild Church of St Martin became Leicester's cathedral in 1927; a medieval church which was rebuilt externally in the late 19th century. Herrick monuments and Richard III memorial.

facilities: ⚒ ♿

100 Kings College Chapel, Cambridgeshire

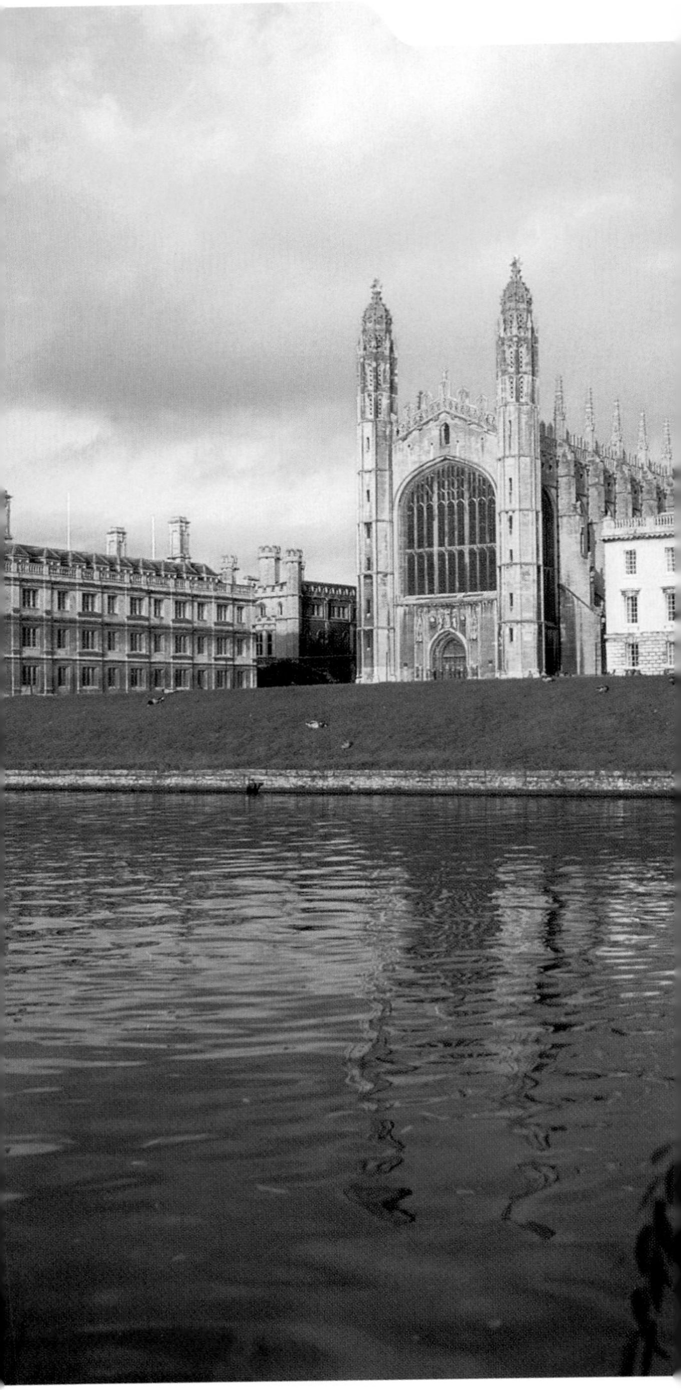

Saint Mary De Castro Church

St Mary De Castro Church, Castle Street, Leicester, LE1 5WN
t: (0116) 262 8727   **w:** smarydecastro.cjb.net

open:	All year, Sat 1400-1700.
description:	The 'Jewel of Leicester's Churches.' Founded in 1107 as a chapel of the Royal Castle; long connections with the Crown. Stunning architecture and glass.
facilities:	⚐ ⊓ ♿

Church of St Mary

Church of St Mary, Burton Street, Melton Mowbray, LE13 1AE
t: (01664) 562267   **w:** melton.leicester.anglican.org

open:	Jan-Dec, Daily 1000-1200, 1400-1600.
description:	The largest parish church in Leicestershire, built between 1170 and 1532, with 40 stained glass windows, a rare candelabra, medieval glass, a fine organ and notable monuments.
facilities:	⌨ ⚐ ♿

STAPLEFORD

Stapleford Saint Mary Magdalene

Stapleford St Mary Magdalene, Sawgate Road, Melton Mowbray, Stapleford, LE14 2SF   t: (020) 7213 0660
w: visitchurches.org.uk

open: Daily 1000-1600.

description: An elegant example of 18thC Gothic Revival architecture, with a tall, gracious tower. The cool, spacious interior features attractive plasterwork, fine oak pews and gallery, and excellent monuments to the Earls of Harborough.

facilities: 🐕

STAUNTON HAROLD

Staunton Harold Church

Staunton Harold Church, Staunton Harold, LE65 1SE
t: (01332) 863822   w: nationaltrust.org.uk

open: Mar-Oct, Sat, Sun 1300-1630. Jun-Aug, Wed-Sun, 1300-1630.

description: One of the very few churches to be built during the Commonwealth period (1655), with original 17thC cushions and hangings, fine panelling and a painted ceiling.

facilities: 💭 🏃 ♿

Saint Botolph's Church

BOSTON

St Botolph's Church, The Parish Office, 1 Wormgate, Boston,
PE21 6NP   **t:** (01205) 362864   **w:** parish-of-boston.org.uk

open: Daily 0830-1630.

description: Known (and visible) far and wide
                    as 'The Stump' a title which strictly
                    belongs to its prodigious 272ft
                    tower, the tallest of any English
                    parish church.

facilities: ▬ 火 丹 ᕋ

Crowland Abbey

CROWLAND

Crowland Abbey, Croyland Abbey, Crowland,
PE6 0EN   **t:** (01733) 211 391
w: crowlandabbey.org.uk

open: All year, Mon-Sat 0900-1700, Sun 1230-1700.

description: Crowland Abbey was founded by St Guthlac
                    in 716AD. It later became one of the nation's
                    most important abbeys with an immense
                    cathedral-sized church and spacious monastic
                    living quarters housing up to 40 Benedictine
                    monks.

facilities: ▬ 火 ᕋ

Saint Andrews Parish Church

St Andrew's Parish Church, Church Walk, Epworth, DN9 1GA
t: (01427) 872080   **w:** standrewsepworth.com

open:	Daily 0900-1600.
description:	Grade I Listed building, 12thC church famous as the church at which Samuel Wesley, father of John and Charles Wesley, was once rector. Many interesting architectural features.
facilities:	⚔ 🪑 ♿

Grantham Saint Wulfram

Grantham St Wulfram, Church Street, Grantham, NG31 6RR
t: (01476) 562334

open:	Apr-Sep, Mon-Sat 0930-1600. Oct-Mar, Mon-Sat 0930-1300.
description:	St. Wulfram's graceful spire, the sixth highest in England, rises to 282ft above Grantham. The church, inside and out, is a noble medieval building of imposing proportions with fine carving, and contains a crypt chapel.
facilities:	💻 ⚔ 🪑 ♿

Lincoln Cathedral

LINCOLN

Lincoln Cathedral, Minster Yard, Lincoln, LN2 1PX
(01522) 561600   **w:** lincolncathedral.com

Open:	Apr-Oct, Mon-Fri 0715-2000, Sat-Sun 0715-1800. Nov-Mar, Mon-Sat 0715-1800, Sun 0715-1700.
Admission:	£4.00
Description:	One of the finest medieval buildings in Europe. High on its hill overlooking the ancient city and dominating the skyline for many miles, it has a visual impact nothing less than startling.
Facilities:	🐾 ⛅ ♿

Lincoln Saint Mary Magdalene

LINCOLN

Lincoln St Mary Magdalene, Castle Hill, Lincoln, LN1 3AR
(01522) 520401   **w:** minstergroup.org

Open:	All year, Mon-Fri 1030-1130. Third Sat in every month 1000-1600.
Description:	The live and active parish church of the ancient city is a place of peace and stillness at the heart of Lincoln's busy tourist area. Explore the church's links with the oldest Christian site in Lincolnshire.
Facilities:	🐕 ⛅ ♿

Louth Saint James

Louth St James, The Rectory, Westgate, Louth, LN11 9YE
t: (01507) 603213   **w:** stjameschurchlouth.com

open: Daily 1030-1600.

description: St. James parish church has the tallest spire,
                at 295ft, of any parish church in the country.
                Built in the 15th century, it is a
                superb example of Perpendicular
                architecture.

facilities:

Sleaford Saint Denys

Sleaford St Denys, The Vicarage, Market Place, Sleaford,
NG34 7SH   **t:** (01529) 302177   **w:** lafforddeanery.org.uk

open: Daily 0845-dusk.

description: 'Nothing about it is dull,' is Simon Jenkins'
                verdict on St. Denys church. Significantly
                restored by famous 19thC church architects
                Kirk and Parry (who were based in the town).
                Loft added by Comper in 1918.

facilities:

Snarford Saint Lawrence

Snarford, St Lawrence, Snarford, LN8 3SL
t: (020) 7213 0660   **w:** visitchurches.org.uk

open: Daily 1000-1600.

description: The treasure of this small medieval church lies
in three wonderful 16th and 17thC monuments
to members of the St Paul family, representing
the evolution from brash Tudor display of
ancestry to elaborate Jacobean symbolism.

facilities:

Spalding St. Mary
& St. Nicholas

Spalding St Mary & St Nicholas, The Parsonage, 1 Halmer
Gate, Spalding, PE11 2DR   **t:** (01775) 722772
w: spaldingchurches.org

open: Daily 0900-1600.

description: One of Spalding's chief glories.
Standing next to Ayscoughfee Hall and near the
River Welland, the church was built in the late 12th
century by the monks of Spalding Priory.

facilities:

Saint Johns Stamford

STAMFORD

St John's Church, St John's Street, Stamford, PE9 2DB
t: (020) 7213 0660   **w:** visitchurches.org.uk

open: Daily.

description: A spacious, 15thC Perpendicular-style
                 church. It has a superb carved roof, and
                 rich furnishings dating from the 15th to 19th
                 centuries. The pews were designed in 1856 by
                 Edward Browning.

facilities: 🐕 ♿

Saint Mary's Church

STOW

Saint Mary's Church, Normanby
Road, Stow, LN1 2DF
t: (01427) 788251
w: stowminster.org.uk

open: All year.

description: One of the most complete Saxon churches
                 surviving in the country, founded c975 with a
                 12thC chancel and one of the largest Saxon
                 arches in the country.

facilities: ☕ 🍴 ♿

Collegiate Church of the Holy Trinity

TATTERSHALL

Collegiate Church of the Holy Trinity, Sleaford Road,
Tattershall   t: (01526) 342223

open: All year, Mon-Sat 0930-1700.

description: Founded in 1439 by Ralph, 3rd Baron
                Cromwell, the Lord High Treasurer of England,
                with an east window of priceless medieval
                glass and a collection of medieval brasses.

facilities: ⬛ 🐕 ⛲ ♿

Birkenhead Priory & St Marys Tower

BIRKENHEAD

Birkenhead Priory & St Marys Tower, Priory Street,
Birkenhead, CH41 5JH   t: (0151) 666 1249
v: wirral.gov.uk/ed/birkenhead_priory.html

open: Apr-Oct, Wed-Fri 1300-1700, Sat-Sun 1000-
                1700, Nov-Mar, Wed-Fri 1200-1600, Sat-Sun
                1000-1600.

description: An ancient monument
                dating back to
                1150. The priory
                site comprises an
                undercroft with
                interpretive display, a chapter house and a
                steeple with 101 steps.

facilities: 🐕 ⛲

Liverpool Anglican Cathedral

Liverpool Anglican Cathedral, St James Mount, Liverpool, L1 7AZ   **t:** (0151) 709 6271
w: liverpoolcathedral.org.uk

open: Daily 0800-1800.

description: The largest cathedral in Britain. A great neo-Gothic building designed by Giles Gilbert Scott, started in 1904 and completed in 1978.

facilities: ▄ 夫 点

Metropolitan Cathedral of Christ the King

Metropolitan Cathedral of Christ the King, Mount Pleasant, Liverpool, L3 5TQ
t: (0151) 709 9222   **w:** liverpoolmetrocathedral.org.uk

open: Daily 0800-1800.

description: A 20thC circular cathedral famous for its 290ft lantern tower, stained glass and modern works of art. Monumental crypt of an earlier incomplete project by Edwin Lutyens.

facilities: ▄ 夫 ⼍ 点

rinces Road Synagogue

rinces Road Synagogue, Synagogue Chambers, Princes
oad, Liverpool, L8 1TG   **t:** (0151) 709 3431
: princesroad.org

pen:　　　　Tours by appointment only, please phone for
　　　　　　details.

escription:　Grade II* listed, with a highly-ornate interior,
　　　　　　this is one of the finest examples of Moorish
　　　　　　Revival synagogue architecture in Europe and
　　　　　　the oldest working synagogue in the North
　　　　　　West.

cilities:　　🗡 ♿

aint Edmund King
nd Martyr

t Edmund King and Martyr (Thatched), Norwich Road, Acle,
R13 3JS   **t:** (01493) 750393   **w:** acle.churchnorfolk.com

pen:　　　　All year, daily.

escription:　This lovely old church, with its beautiful
　　　　　　thatched and slate roof, is about 1100 years
　　　　　　old. Its round tower (thought to be Saxon)
　　　　　　houses six bells, dating back to 1623.

cilities:　　🗡 🏓 ♿

Saint Mary the Virgin

St Mary the Virgin (Thatched), Beachamwell
t: (01366) 348063   **w:** stmarysbeachamwell.co.uk

open: All year.

description: A pretty thatched church in a picturesque
                   village setting. A 15thC octagonal top
                   augments its Saxon round tower. Do not miss
                   the cast iron chest and intriguing graffiti.

facilities:

Binham Priory

Binham Priory, Binham, NR21 ODW
t: (01328) 830362   **w:** binhampriory.org.uk

open: All year.

description: Extensive remains of an early 12thC
                   Benedictine priory. The west front is a fine
                   example of Early English architecture and the
                   original nave is still used as the parish church.

facilities:

Booton Saint Michael the Archangel

Booton, St Michael the Archangel, Church Road, Booton,
NR10 4NZ   t: (020) 7213 0660   w: visitchurches.org.uk

open:	Daily 1000-1600.
description:	An extraordinary building, the product of one man's eccentric imagination. Built by Whitwell Elwin in the late 19th century, it borrows details from other churches throughout the country, but the slender twin towers are entirely original.
facilities:	🐕

Castle Acre Priory

Castle Acre Priory, Stocks Green, Castle Acre,
PE32 2AF   t: (01760) 755394
w: english-heritage.org.uk

open:	Apr-Sep, daily 1000-1800. Oct-Mar, Mon, Thu-Sun 1000-1600.
admission:	£4.70

description: Romantic and atmospheric Cluniac priory with a 12thC church, prior's lodgings, beautiful 12thC west front, gatehouse and recreated medieval herb garden to enjoy.

facilities:	🐕 ♿

Saint Mary

St Mary (Thatched), Lynn Road, Cranwich, IP26 5JL
t: (01842) 878220
w: norfolkchurches.co.uk/cranwich/cranwich.htm

open: All year.

description: Small thatched church full of atmosphere. The Saxon tower has unusual sound holes and the slightly later addition of battlements and gargoyles. Don't miss the Victorian harmonium boasting mouse-proof pedals.

facilities: 🐕

Saint Edmund

St Edmund (Thatched), Fritton, NR31 9EZ
t: (01493) 488345   **w:** paintedchurch.org/frited.htm

open: Mar-Dec, daily.

description: This thatched church with its round tower and apsidal chancel was widened in the 14th century creating an unusual off-centre layout. Don't miss the early wall paintings and triple-decker pulpit.

facilities: 🐕 ♿

Saint Mary

St Mary (Thatched), Church Lane, West Somerton, Great
Yarmouth, NR29 4DP   **t:** (01493) 668762
w: norfolkchurches.co.uk/somertonwest/somertonwest.htm

open: All year, please contact keyholder for access.

description: A medieval church with a Norman tower and
thatched nave. The 13thC wall paintings and
19thC grave of Robert Hales, the Norfolk
Giant, make this a must see.

facilities: ⚐ ⊼ ♿

Hales Saint Margaret

Hales St Margaret, Church Lane, Hales, NR14 6QL
t: (020) 7213 0660   **w:** visitchurches.org.uk

open: Daily 1000-1600.

description: This little church
in open countryside is an
almost perfect Norman
building with round tower,
semicircular apse and
thatched roof. The north
and south doorways are
magnificently carved. Fine Norman stonework inside.

facilities: 🐕

Shell Museum and Saint Martins Church

Shell Museum and Saint Martins Church, Glandford, Holt, NR25 7JR   **t:** (01263) 740081   **w:** shellmuseum.org.uk

open:	Church Daily. Museum Tue-Sat, Bank Hols 1000-1230, 1400-1630.
admission:	£2.00
description:	The museum has exhibits of shells, fossils, pottery and objects of local history. The church has beautiful carvings and a clock with a 12-bell carillon.
facilities:	⍝ ⊼ ♿

Shirehall Museum and Abbey Gardens

Shirehall Museum and Abbey Gardens, Common Place, Little Walsingham, NR22 6BP   **t:** (01328) 820510

open:	Apr-Nov, Feb-Mar, daily 1000-1630. Dec, Sat-Sun 1000-1630.
admission:	£3.00
description:	A Georgian country courthouse, local museum and Tourist Information Centre. Ruins of the Augustinian abbey, peaceful gardens and woodland walks, set in approximately 20 acres.
facilities:	⍝ ⊼ ♿

Saint Benets Abbey

St Benets Abbey, Horning, Ludham
w: norfarchtrust.org.uk

open: All year.

description: The ruins of a monastery founded in
1020 by King Canute. A gatehouse with
interesting carvings, 18thC windmill tower
and a perimeter wall around the 34 acres with
fishponds.

facilities: 🏇 ⛩ ♿

Saint Peter and St Paul

St Peter and St Paul (Thatched), Mautby Lane, Mautby,
NR29 3JA   **t:** (01493) 730122   **w:** mautby.churchnorfolk.com

open: All year, please contact keyholder for access.

description: This well-preserved thatched church with
round tower is the burial place of Margaret
Paston, author of many of the Paston letters
detailing life during the Wars of the Roses.

facilities: 🐕 ♿

Norwich Cathedral

Norwich Cathedral, 62 The
Close, Norwich, NR1 4EH
t: (01603) 218321
w: cathedral.org.uk

open: May-Sep, daily 0700-1800.
Oct-Apr, daily 0730-1800.
admission: £4.30

description: A Norman cathedral
from 1096 with 14thC roof bosses
depicting bible scenes from Adam
and Eve to the Day of Judgement. Cloisters, cathedral close,
shop and restaurant.

facilities:

Roman Catholic Cathedral of St John The Baptist

Roman Catholic Cathedral of St John The Baptist, Unthank
Road, Norwich, NR2 2PA   **t:** (01603) 624615
w: stjohncathedral.co.uk

open: Daily 0700-2000.

description: A particularly fine example of 19thC Gothic
revival by George Gilbert Scott Junior, with
fine stained glass, exquisite stonewalk and
Frosterley marble.

facilities:

Saint Peter Mancroft Church

Saint Peter Mancroft Church, Haymarket, Norwich, NR2 1QX
t: (01603) 610443   **w:** stpetermancroft.org.uk

open: All year, Mon-Sat 1000-1600.

description: A church with a Norman foundation (1075).
                   The present church was consecrated in 1455
                   and features font (1463), Flemish tapestry
                   (1573), east window with medieval glass and
                   Thomas Browne memorial.

facilities: ▆ 🏃 ⛩ ♿

Thetford Priory

Thetford Priory, Thetford
t: (01223) 582766   **w:** english-heritage.org.uk

open: All year.

description: The 14thC gatehouse is the best preserved
                   part of this Cluniac priory, built in 1103.
                   The extensive remains include a plan of the
                   cloisters.

facilities: 🐕 ♿

Walpole St Peter's Church

WALPOLE ST PETER

Walpole St Peter's Church, Church Road, Walpole St Peter,
PE14 7NS   **t:** (01945) 780206
w: ely.anglican.org/parishes/walpole-st-peter

open: Daily.

description: A masterpiece of 14thC architecture. Famous
                   annual flower festival.

facilities: 🐕 ⛱ ♿

Shrine of our Lady of Walsingham

WALSINGHAM

Shrine of our Lady of Walsingham, Holt Road, Walsingham,
NR22 6BW   **t:** (01328) 820239

open: Daily, dawn-dusk.

description: A pilgrimage church containing the Holy
                   House, standing in extensive grounds.

facilities: 🐕 ♿

WALSINGHAM

Slipper Chapel: Roman Catholic National Shrine

Slipper Chapel: Roman Catholic National Shrine, Houghton St Giles, Walsingham, NR22 6AL

: (01328) 820217   **w:** walsingham.org.uk

Open: Daily, dawn-dusk.

Description: The Roman Catholic National Shrine of Our Lady. A small 14thC chapel. Plus the new Chapel of Reconciliation. Bookshop and tearoom.

Facilities: ▆ ⚲ ⊓ ♿

WYMONDHAM

Wymondham Abbey

Wymondham Abbey, Vicar Street, Wymondham, NR18 0PL

: (01953) 602269   **w:** wymondhamabbey.nildram.co.uk

open: Apr, Mon-Sat 1000-1600. May-Oct, Mon-Sat 1000-1700. Nov, Mon-Sat 1000-1600. Dec-Mar, Mon-Sat 1000-1500.

Description: Magnificent Norman church, built 1107, with ruins of former Benedictine abbey. Splendid interior with angel roofs, two 18thC organs and gold-faced reredos. Shop on site.

Facilities: ▆ ⚔ ⊓ ♿

Saint Laurence's Church

ALDFIELD

St Laurence's Church, Aldfield, HG4 3BE
t: (01765) 601167   **w:** aldfieldchurch.co.uk

open: All year.

description: A church dedicated to St Laurence has stood on this site since 1344, although the present building dates from c1782. Listed in Simon Jenkins' book, 'England's Thousand Best Churches'.

facilities: ⚔ ♿

Priory Church of St Maryand St Cuthb

BOLTON ABBEY

The Priory Church of St Maryand St Cuthb, The Church Office, Bolton Abbey, BD23 6AL
t: (01756) 710326   **w:** boltonpriory.org.uk

open: Daily 0800-1630.

description: Living church in the 13thC nave of a 12thC Augustinian priory. The south windows are by Pugin. Victorian wall painting. Substantial ruins.

facilities: 🐕 ⛩ ♿

Byland Abbey (EH)

COXWOLD

Byland Abbey (English Heritage), Coxwold, YO61 4BD
t: (01904) 601974   **w:** english-heritage.org.uk

Open: See website for details.
Admission: £3.00

Description: Once one of the great northern monasteries,
                  Byland Abbey's design influenced many other
                  religious buildings throughout
                  Europe. The abbey contains a
                  splendid collection of medieval
                  floor tiles.

Facilities: 🐕 ⛩ ♿

Saint Mary Magdalene's Church

HELMSLEY

St Mary Magdalene's Church, East Moors, Helmsley
t: (01439) 770236   **w:** helmsleydeanery.org/
eastmoorschurch.html

Open: Daily, dawn-dusk.

description: A wonderful church hidden deep in
the North York Moors. Its painted wagon roof
and lavish decoration by Temple Moore, have
delighted and inspired both Sir John Betjeman
and Pevsner.

Facilities: 🐕

Saint Gregorys Minster

KIRKBYMOORSID

St Gregory's Minster, Kirkdale, Kirkbymoorside, YO62 6NN
t: (01439) 771609

open:	All year, daily 0930-1500 winter summer 0930 1800.
description:	Saxon church with unique Saxon sundial, 7th Celtic crosses and carved stones.
facilities:	ㅐ 큐 ♿

Saint Mary's Church

LASTINGHAM

St Mary's Church, Lastingham, YO62 6TN
t: (01751) 417344   **w:** lastinghamchurch.org.uk

open:	Daily, dawn-dusk.
description:	The church stands on the site of a 7thC Celtic monastery, founded by St Cedd, of Lindisfarne. The existing building dates from 1078. Don't miss the unique apsidical Norman crypt.
facilities:	ㅐ ♿

EDDI

S. Cædmon

St Oswald King

Saint Mary's Priory

OLD MALTON

St Mary's Priory, Town Street, Old Malton,
YO17 7HB   **t:** (01653) 692121

open: Daily 0900-1700.

description: The last Gilbertine priory in use for worship
in England. Norman architecture, interesting
archaeological remains, finely carved
misericords, Victorian church furnishings.

facilities:

Saint Mary's Church

REDMIRE

St Mary's Church, Redmire
t: 01969 624604

open: Daily, dawn-dusk.

description: At nearly 900 years old, St Mary's is the
quintessential English country church.
Affording breathtaking views across
Wensleydale to Pen Hill, this church gives a
fascinating insight into past customs.

facilities:

Easby Abbey

Easby Abbey, Richmond
0870 333 1181   **w:** english-heritage.org.uk

Open: Apr-Sep, Daily 1000-1800, Oct, Daily 1000-
                    1700, Nov-Mar, Daily 1000-1600.

Description: The substantial remains of the 12thC medieval
                    abbey buildings stand in a beautiful setting
                    by the River Swale near Richmond. The
                    gatehouse is little altered since the 14th
                    century.

Facilities: 🐕 🏓

Rievaulx Abbey (EH)

Rievaulx Abbey (English Heritage), Rievaulx,
O62 5LB   **t:** (01904) 601974
: english-heritage.org.uk

Open: See website for details.
Admission: £4.20

Description: Experience the beauty of this impressive
                    monastic site. It was the first Cistercian abbey
                    to be founded in northern England, and one of
                    the most powerful abbeys in Europe.

Facilities: 🐕 🏓 ♿

RIPON

Fountains Abbey and Studley Royal

Fountains Abbey and Studley Royal Water Garden, Ripon, HG4 3DY   **t:** (01765) 608888   **w:** fountainsabbey.org.uk

open:	Mar-Oct, daily 1000-1700. Nov-Feb, daily 1000-1600.
admission:	£6.50
description:	The largest monastic ruin in Britain, founded by Cistercian monks in 1132. Landscaped garden laid 1720-1740 with lake, formal water garden, temples and deer park.
facilities:	☕ 🐕 ⛱ ♿

RIPON

Jervaulx Abbey

Jervaulx Abbey, Park House, Jervaulx, Ripon, HG4 4PH
t: (01677) 460226   **w:** jervaulxabbey.com

open:	All year, dawn-dusk.
admission:	£2.00
description:	A ruined Cistercian abbey, set in 110 acres of parkland noted for its lovely wallflowers and shrubs. The informal grounds give a true feeling of tranquillity and serenity.
facilities:	☕ 🐕 ⛱ ♿

Ripon Cathedral

Ripon Cathedral, Ripon, HG4 1PE
(01765) 604108   **w:** ripon-cathedral.org.uk

Open: Daily 0800-1800.

Description: Founded by St Wilfrid in 672AD, Ripon
           Cathedral, as it stands today, is the inheritor of
           over 1,300 years of history and worship.

Facilities: 🚹 ♿

Selby Abbey

Selby Abbey, The Crescent, Selby, YO8 4PU
(01757) 703123   **w:** selbyabbey.org.uk

Open: All year, daily 1000-1600.

description: The abbey's foundations date back
to 1069. It is probably the most outstanding
example of a monastic abbey in the north of
England. Architectural features include Norman
arches.

Facilities: 🚹 ♿

All Saints Church

All Saints Church, Sherburn in Elmet, LS25 6AX
t: (01977) 682122   **w:** allsaintschurchsherburninelmet.org

open: All year, daily. If locked, please contact the vicarage or church wardens.

description: This Perpendicular-style church incorporates earlier Saxon and Norman elements. The 13thC chancel is a good example of Early English style ecclesiastical architecture. Don't miss the rare 15thC Janus Cross.

facilities: 🐕 ♿

Saint Giles' Church

St Giles' Church, Skelton, YO30 1XT
t: (01904) 470045

open: Daily, dawn-dusk.

description: This Grade I Listed church is one of the most complete examples of a 13th century English parish church in existence. Built around 1240 by masons employed on York Minster.

facilities: 🐕 ♿

Mount Grace Priory (EH/NT)

STADDLEBRIDGE

Mount Grace Priory (EH/NT), Staddlebridge, DL6 3JG
t: (01904) 601974   **w:** english-heritage.org.uk

open: Apr-Sep, Thu_Mon 1000-1800, Oct-Mar, Thu-Sun 1000-1600.

admission: £4.00

description: The best-preserved example of the ten British charterhouses where Carthusian monks lived as hermits. Founded in 1398. Remains include a restored two-storey monk's cell.

facilities: 🐕 ⛱ ♿

Church of St Mary the Virgin

WHITBY

The Church of St Mary the Virgin, Whitby
t: (0113) 244 3413

open: Mar-Oct, Mon-Sat 1000-1600, Sun 1200-1600. Nov-Dec weather dependent. Please phone for details.

description: This Norman church with unusual Georgian windows is dramatically situated on the cliff top beside the Gothic ruins of Whitby Abbey. The interior is crammed with galleries and box pews.

facilities: 🚫 ♿

Whitby Abbey

Whitby Abbey, Whitby, YO22 4JT
t: (01904) 601974   **w:** english-heritage.org.uk

open:	See website for details.
admission:	£4.20

description: The moody and magnificent Whitby Abbey has drawn successive generations to this site of settlement, and has been responsible for religious devotion and even literary inspiration.

facilities: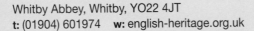

Kirkham Priory (EH)

Kirkham Priory (English Heritage), Whitwell-on-the-Hill, YO60 7JS   **t:** (01904) 601974   **w:** english-heritage.org.uk

open:	See website for details.
admission:	£3.00

description: The ruins of this Augustinian priory, set in the peaceful Derwent valley, include a magnificent carved gatehouse, declaring to the world the priory's association with the rich and powerful

facilities: ⚐ ⛺ ♿

Saint Michael-le-Belfrey (Minster Yard)

YORK

St Michael-le-Belfrey (Minster Yard), York,
YO1 7HH   **t:** (01904) 624190
w: stmichaelsyork.org

open: Daily 1000-1600.

description: Standing next to York Minster on the
alignment of the ancient Roman fortress Via
Principia, St Michael-le-Belfrey is the only pre-
Reformation church in York to have been built
all at one time, between 1525 and 1536.

facilities: ⚲ ♿

York Minster

YORK

York Minster, Deangate, York, YO1 7HH
t: (01904) 557216   **w:** yorkminster.org

open: All year, Mon-Sat 0900-1700, Sun 1200-1545.
admission: £5.00

description: The largest medieval Gothic
cathedral in northern Europe,
and a treasure house of
800 years of stained glass.
Experience York's finest
viewpoint from the top of the central tower's
275 steps.

facilities: ☕ 🐕 ⛩ ♿

All Saints Church

All Saints Church, Church Street, Brixworth
t: (01604) 880286   **w:** friendsofbrixworthchurch.org.uk

open: Daily, dawn-dusk.

description: One of the finest Anglo-Saxon churches in the
                  country with mostly original 7thC work and
                  much Roman material. The tower and stair
                  turret were added in the 10th century.

facilities:

Saint Margaret of Antioch, Crick

St Margaret of Antioch, Crick, Church Street, Crick, NN6 7TP
t: (01788) 822147

open: Daily.

description: Mentioned in the Domesday Book, there has
                  been worship on this site for 1,000 years. One
                  of 'England's Thousand Best Churches.'

facilities:

Church of All Saints — EARLS BARTON

Church of All Saints, Earls Barton, NN6 0JG
t: (01604) 810447   w: allsaintsearlsbarton.org.uk

open: Apr-Oct, Mon-Sat 1030-1230, 1400-1600.

description: A fine Anglo-Saxon stone tower in four stages with a Norman arch in the main porch and Norman arcading in the choir area.

facilities: 🐕

Saint Peter's East Carlton — EAST CARLTON

St Peter's East Carlton, Church Lane, East Carlton, LE16 8YA
t: (01536) 771396

open: Please contact keyholder for access, details on the noticeboard.

description: Originally 13thC, but largely 18thC. The church contains an important monument to Sir Geoffrey Palmer, Attorney General to King Charles II.

facilities: 🐕 🪑

Church Saint Mary

Church of St Mary & All Saints, Fotheringhay
t: (01832) 226243

open:	Daily 1000-1800.
description:	Although not as large as it was in the 15th century, this magnificent church with an unusual octagonal lantern tower dominates the countryside. It has a beautiful 15thC pulpit.
facilities:	🐕 ⛩ ♿

Saint Mary's Great Brington

St Mary's Great Brington, Main Street, Great Brington, NN7 4JD **t:** (01604) 770402

open:	Apr-Oct, Sat-Sun, Bank Hols 1400-1700, Jul-Sep, Daily 1400-1700.
description:	Beautiful church with fine pew ends, the tomb of an ancestor of George Washington, and Spencer Chapel where generations of the Spencer family are buried.
facilities:	🐕

Saint Mary Magdalene

St Mary Magdalene, Helmdon, Church Street, Helmdon,
NN13 5QJ   **t:** (01604) 770402

open: Daily, dawn-dusk.

description: This church was built during the 13th and 14th
                  centuries. There is an early English piscine and
                  sedilia with serious and comic carvings. Also a
                  magnificent 2000-year-old yew.

facilities:

Chichele College

Chichele College, Higham Ferrers
t: (01933) 314157   **w:** english-heritage.org.uk

open: Please contact keyholder for access.

description: Founded as a college for secular canons
                  in 1422 by Henry Chichele, Archbishop
                  of Canterbury. Parts of a quadrangle
                  incorporating a chapel and Bede House still
                  remain.

facilities:

All Saints Northampton

NORTHAMPTON

All Saints Northampton, George Row, Northampton, NN7 4JD
t: (01604) 632194

open: All year, Mon-Fri 0915-1400.

description: Grade I Listed fine 17thC interior, plaster work by Edward Goudge, Christopher Wren's chief plasterer. Choral music six days a week, cafe open daily.

facilities:

Church of the Holy Sepulchre

NORTHAMPTON

Church of the Holy Sepulchre, Sheep Street, Northampton, NN1 3NL **t:** (01604) 754782

open: May-Sep Wed 1200-1600. Sat 1400-1600.

description: The largest Norman round church in England, from c1100 with a tower from c1300. Naves, a Gilbert Scott restoration, Crusader window and Northamptonshire Regiment memorial chapel.

facilities:

See pages 2-3 for key to symbols

Delapre Abbey

Delapre Abbey, London Road, Northampton, NN4 8AW
t: (01604) 708675   **w:** delapreabbey.org

open: Daily 1000-1700.

description: A 17thC house on the site of a 12thC nunnery,
                   and set in one of the most beautiful public
                   gardens in Northampton. Traces of the original
                   medieval buildings remain.

facilities: ☕ 🐕 ⛱ ♿

Holy Trinity Church Rothwell

Holy Trinity Church Rothwell, High Street, Rothwell,
NN14 6BQ   **t:** (01536) 710268   **w:** rothwellholytrinity.co.uk

open: All year, Wed 1000-1200, Apr-Sun, Sun 1430-
                   1630.

description: Holy Trinity Church has the longest
nave in the county. The main body of the church
dates from the 13th century although the oldest
part was built in Norman times.

facilities: 🐕 ⛱ ♿

Parish Church of All Hallows

The Parish Church of All Hallows, Church Street,
Wellingborough, NN8 5AQ   **t:** (01933) 222002
w: allhallowswellingborough.com

open: All year, Tue-Sat 1000-1200.

description: All Hallows is the ancient parish church of
Wellingborough. It stands on the site of an
earlier pre-Conquest building, but the oldest
existing feature
is the splendid
Norman doorway
in the south porch
dating from c1150.

facilities: 🍴 🐕 ♿

Saint Aidans

St Aidan's, Bamburgh
t: (01668) 214748   **w:** bamburgh.org.uk

open: All year, daily 0800-dusk.

description: St Aidan founded a church on the site in 635
although the present building is 13th century.
It overlooks the spectacular Bamburgh Castle
and the North Sea.

facilities: 🐕 ♿

Lindisfarne Priory

BERWICK-UPON-TWEED

Lindisfarne Priory, Holy Island, Berwick-upon-Tweed,
TD15 2RX   **t:** (01289) 389200   **w:** english-heritage.org.uk

open: Apr-Sep, Daily 0930-1700,
Oct, Daily 0930-1600, Nov-Jan, Mon,
Sat-Sun 1000-1400, Feb-Mar, Daily
1000-1600.
admission: £3.90

description: Founded in AD635,
Lindisfarne, now an impressive ruin, is
considered the birthplace of Christianity
in Britain. The dramatic approach
across the causeway adds to the fascination of the site.

facilities: 🐕 ♿

Saint Andrew's Church

BOLAM

St Andrew's Church, Bolam, NE61 3UX
t: (01661) 881654

open: Daily 0900-1700.

description: A gem of a church noted for its late-Saxon
                   tower, Norman moulded chancel arch and the
                   Short Flat Chapel.

facilities: 🐕 ♿

Shotley, St. Andrew

Shotley, St Andrew, Greymare Hill, Consett, DH8 9SJ
t: (020) 7213 0660   **w:** visitchurches.org.uk

open: Daily 1000-1600.

description: Built in 1769, almost 300m above sea level, to a cruciform plan on the site of a medieval church, and remodelled in 1892. Churchyard contains magnificent domed mausoleum built by Humphrey Hopper in 1752.

facilities: 🐕

Hexham Abbey

Hexham Abbey, Beaumont Street, Hexham, NE46 3NB
t: (01434) 602031   **w:** hexhamabbey.org.uk

open: Daily 0930-1700.
admission: £3.00

description: Saxon crypt, 15thC paintings, misericords
                   and Saxon chalice, 7thC Frith stool and
                   Augustinian night stair. Most of the church is in
                   the Early English style of architecture.

facilities: 🍴 ♿

HOLY ISLAND

indisfarne Heritage Centre

ndisfarne Heritage Centre, Marygate, Holy Island,
015 2SD   **t:** (01289) 389004
: lindisfarne-heritage-centre.org

pen: Apr-Oct, daily 1000-1700. Nov-Mar, please
                check with the Centre.

escription: A centre designed to provide a valuable and
                unique sociological and historical link between
                Lindisfarne past and present. Includes
                exhbitions of the Lindisfarne Gospels and
                island life.

cilities: 🐕 ♿

LONGFRAMLINGTON

rinkburn Priory

rinkburn Priory, Longframlington, NE65 8AR
(01665) 570628   **w:** english-heritage.org.uk

pen: See website for details.
dmission: £2.70

escription: Founded in 1135, the
                priory was restored in the
                19th century, and now
                survives in its entirety as
                Northumberland's finest
                example of early Gothic architecture.

cilities: 🐕 🪑

Saint Andrews Church

St Andrew's Church, Hartburn, Morpeth, NE61 4JB
t: (01670) 775360

open: Daily 0900-1700.

description: Eleventh-century church used by the
Knights Templar. Cromwell's money box and
Peninsular War flags. John Hodgson, the
historian, is buried here.

facilities:

Saint Lawrence Church

St Lawrence Church, Dial Place, Warkworth, Morpeth,
NE65 0UR   **t:** (01665) 711217   **w:** stlawrence-church.org.uk

open: All year, dawn-dusk.

description: A Norman church built on Saxon foundations.
Later additions include the 13thC tower, 14thC
spire and late-15thC south aisle. At 90ft, it has
the longest Norman nave in Northumberland.

facilities:

Saint Mary Magdalene's Church

St Mary Magdalene's Church, The Rectory, Whalton, Morpeth, NE61 3UX   t: (01670) 775360

open: Daily 0730-1700.

description: Largely medieval church displaying the
                   evolution of a well-developed 13thC church
                   from a Norman core. Carvings in stonework
                   and a turret clock dated 1796.

facilities: 🐕 ♿

Saint Peters Church

St Peters Church, Lincoln House, Clayworth, DN22 9AD
t: (01777) 817688   w: stpetersclayworth.org

open: All year, daily.

description: Home to the largest single
                   work of art in the East of
                   England - the spectacular
                   Traquair Murals, by Scottish
                   artist Phoebe Anna Traquair
                   (1852-1936), which cover all
                   four walls.

facilities: 🐕 ♿

Church of St Mary

Church of St Mary, Church Street, Edwinstowe, NG21 9QA
t: (01623) 822430

open: Daily 0900-1600.

description: The 12th-15thC church where Robin Hood is
supposed to have married Maid Marian, with
a 12thC pillar piscina, a forest measure and a
14thC chantry altar.

facilities: ⚞ ♿

Church of St Mary the Virgin

Church of St Mary the Virgin, High Pavement, The
Lacemarket, Nottingham, NG1 1HF   **t:** (0115) 958 2105
w: stmarysnottingham.org

open: All year, Tue-Sun 1000-1500.

description: The civic church of Nottingham, in the
Lacemarket. A 15thC church in Perpendicular
style with a central tower on the site of older
churches and a 1973 Marcussen organ.

facilities: ⚟ ⛩ ♿

NOTTINGHAMSHIRE 147

Saint Mary Magdalene Church

NOTTINGHAM

St Mary Magdalene Church, Market Place, Hucknall,
Nottingham, NG15 7FQ   **t:** (0115) 963 4385

open: All year, Mon-Tue 1000-1200,
1400-1600, Wed 1000-1200,
Thu 1000-1200, 1400-1600,
Fri 1000-1500, Sat 1000-1200,
1400-1600.

description: Set in peaceful churchyard in centre of busy
town. Tower built between the 12th and 14th
centuries, porch in 1320. The building seen
today is the result of restoration work begun in
1872.

facilities: 🐕 ⛉ ♿

Newstead Abbey

RAVENSHEAD

Newstead Abbey, Newstead Abbey Park, Ravenshead,
NG15 8NA   **t:** (01623) 455900

open: Park: All year, daily 0900-dusk. Abbey: Apr-
Sep, daily 1200-1700.
admission: £3.00

description: The 800-year-old
remains of a priory church,
converted into a country
house in the 16th century;
the home of Lord Byron with
possessions, manuscripts,
parkland, a lake and gardens.

facilities: 🖥 🐕 ⛉ ♿

Southwell Minster

Southwell Minster, The Minster Office, The Minster Centre,
Church Street, Southwell, NG25 0HD
t: (01636) 817282   **w:** southwellminster.org.uk

open:	Mar-Oct, daily 0800-1900. Nov-Feb, daily 0800-dusk.
admission:	£3.00
description:	Southwell Minster is a superb cathedral and minster church with one of the finest Norman naves in Europe.
facilities:	

Priory Church of Our Lady and St Cuthbert

Priory Church of Our Lady and St Cuthbert, Priorswell Road,
Worksop, S80 2HX   **t:** (01909) 472180
w: worksoppriory.co.uk

open:	All year, Sat 0900-1200.
description:	A pre-Conquest church with a two-tower facade rebuilt in 1103 with a unique transitional Norman nave, a 12thC Gothic lady chapel and a 1341 gatehouse with chapel.
facilities:	

Gurdwara Sri Guru Singh Sabha

SOUTHALL

Gurdwara Sri Guru Singh Sabha, Havelock Road, Southall,
UB2 4NP   **t:** (020) 8574 4311   **w:** sgsss.org

open: Daily 0530-2130.

description: Europe's biggest Sikh temple, finished in
               marble and granite with a gilded dome and
               stained glass windows.

facilities: ⚗ ♿

Abingdon Abbey

ABINGDON

Abingdon Abbey, Abbey Buildings, 18 Thames Street,
Abingdon, OX14 3HZ   **t:** (01235) 525339
w: friendsofabingdon.org.uk

open: Apr-Sep, Tue-Sun 1400-1600.
admission: £1.00

description: Range of medieval domestic buildings
               remaining from Abingdon Abbey.

facilities: 🐕 ⛩ ♿

Saint Mary's Church

St Mary's Church, Horse Fair, Banbury, OX16 0AA
t: (01295) 253329   **w:** stmaryschurch.banbury.org.uk

open: Apr-Oct, Mon-Sat 1000-1600, Nov-Mar, Fri 1100-1500, Sat 1000-1600.

description: Historic town centre church built in 1797. Many unusual features inside and out.

facilities: 🐕 ⛩ ♿

Saint Johns Church

St John's Church, Church Green, Burford, OX18 4RY
t: (01993) 823788   **w:** burfordchurch.org

open: Summer: daily 0900-1700. Winter: daily, 0900-1600.

description: An impressive cathedral-like church which dates back to around 1175 and took more than 300 years to build. It has many beautiful artefacts and fascinating historical stories.

facilities: 🚶 ♿

Abbey and Cloister Gallery

DORCHESTER ON THAMES

Abbey and Cloister Gallery, Dorchester on Thames, OX10 7HH
t: (01865) 340007
w: dorchester-abbey.org.uk

open: Daily 0800-1800.

description: A parish church, formerly an abbey. The present building dates from the 12th to 14th centuries. Besides the abbey, the small museum houses a display of artefacts illustrating Dorchester's history.

facilities: ☕ 🐕 ⛱ ♿

Christ Church

OXFORD

Christ Church, St Aldate's, Oxford, OX1 1DP
t: (01865) 276492   **w:** chch.ox.ac.uk

open: All year, Mon-Sat 0900-1700, Sun 1300-1700.
admission: £4.70

description: The largest college in Oxford with a cathedral within its walls. The home of Lewis Carroll and Alice in Wonderland.

facilities: 🚶 ♿

OXFORD

Saint Michael at the North Gate

Saint Michael at the North Gate, Church Tower, Cornmarket Street, Oxford, OX1 3EY   **t:** (01865) 255770   **w:** smng.org.uk

open:	Apr-Oct, Mon-Sat 1030-1700. Sun 1200-1600. Nov-Mar. Mon-Sat 1030-1600, Sun 1200-1600.
admission:	£1.80
description:	Oxford's oldest building, boasting the oldest stained glass in Oxford. Associated with William Shakespeare, William Morris and Charles I.
facilities:	

ACTON BURNELL

Langley Chapel and Gatehouse

Langley Chapel and Gatehouse, Acton Burnell, SY5 7PE
t: (0121) 625 6820   **w:** english-heritage.org.uk

open:	Mar-Oct, Daily 1000-1700. Nov-Feb, daily 1000-1600.
description:	Small 17thC chapel remarkable for its early 17thC wooden fittings and furnishings.
facilities:	

Saint Bartholomew Church

St Bartholomew Church, Richard's Castle, Ludlow, SY8 1AY
t: (020) 7213 0660   **w:** visitchurches.org.uk

open: Daily 1000-1600.

description: Spectacular setting next to an early 'marcher castle.' Detached bell tower. The unrestored interior, with a chantry chapel for the Knight Templars of St John, and a superb 17thC canopied pew, is timeless and atmospheric.

facilities: 🐕

Saint Laurences Ludlow

St Laurence's, Ludlow
t: (01584) 872073   **w:** stlaurences.org.uk

open: Apr-Dec, Mon-Sat 1000-1730, Sun 1230-1730. Jan-Mar, Mon-Sat 1100-1600, Sun after morning services until 1600.

description: An impressive cathedral-like church, largely rebuilt in the 15th century in perpendicular style. It has an impressive 132ft square tower, a hexagonal porch and houses many interesting carvings and features.

facilities: 🧗 ⛩ ♿

Holy Trinity Church

Holy Trinity Church, Willmore Street, Much Wenlock,
TF13 6HR   **t:** (01952) 727396   **w:** wenlockchurches.co.uk

open: Jan-Dec, Mon-Sun 0900-1700.

description: Medieval church and churchyard within centre
of ancient market town of Much Wenlock.
Memorial to William Penny Brookes (rebirth of
Olympic Games). Memorial to Mary Webb.

facilities:

Lilleshall Abbey

Lilleshall Abbey, Lilleshall, Newport, TF10 9HW
t: (0121) 625 6820   **w:** english-heritage.org.uk

open: Apr-Sep, Mon-Sun 1000-1700.

description: Established c1148 by Richard de Belmeis for
canons from Dorchester Abbey in Oxfordshire.
Church not completed until 13th century.
Notable west front doorway.

facilities:

Shrewsbury Abbey

SHREWSBURY

Shrewsbury Abbey, Abbey Foregate, Shrewsbury, SY2 6BS
t: (01743) 232723   **w:** shrewsburyabbey.com

open: Apr-Oct, daily 1000-1600. Nov-Mar, Mon-Sat 1030-1500, Sun 1100-1430.

description: The abbey was founded in 1083 by the Norman Roger de Montgomery. The Chronicles of Brother Cadfael, written by Ellis Peters, are inspired by medieval Shrewsbury.

facilities:

Bath Abbey

BATH

Bath Abbey, Abbey Church Yard, Bath, BA1 1LT
t: (01225) 422462   **w:** bathabbey.org

open: Apr-Oct, daily 0900-1800. Nov-Mar, daily 0900-1630.
admission: £2.50

description: Late 15thC abbey built on the site of a Saxon and Norman abbey. Magnificent example of the Perpendicular period of English Gothic architecture. Display in vaults.

facilities:

Glastonbury Abbey

Glastonbury Abbey, Abbey Gatehouse, Magdalen
Street, Glastonbury, BA6 9EL   **t:** (01458) 832267
w: glastonburyabbey.com

open:	Mar-May, Sep-Nov 0930-1800 (or dusk if earlier). Jun-Aug 0900-1800. Dec-Feb 1000-18.00.
admission:	£4.50
description:	Magnificent abbey ruins and grounds. The legendary burial place of King Arthur. With a modern museum, living history presentations and outdoor summer café. Grounds include an orchard and ornamental lake.
facilities:	

Muchelney Abbey

Muchelney Abbey, Muchelney, TA10 0DQ
t: (01458) 250664   **w:** english-heritage.org.uk/muchelney

open:	See website for details.
admission:	£3.20
description:	The abbey was first established by Ine, a 7thC King of Wessex. The Abbot's lodging is the best preserved feature of the abbey.
facilities:	

Oare Church -
St Mary's Church

Oare Church - St Mary's Church, Oare,
EX35 6NX   **t:** 0845 660 3232

open: Please phone for details.

description: Set in the beautiful wooded
valley of Oare Water, the church
was the scene of Lorna Doone's wedding in
the novel by R D Blackmore.

facilities: ✗

Culbone Church -
St Beuno

Culbone Church - St Beuno, Culbone, Porlock
t: (01643) 863150

open: Daily.

description: This Exmoor parish church
is the smallest in England where regular
worship is still offered. Its dimensions are
35ft by 12ft.

facilities: ✗

Downside Abbey

STRATTON-ON-THE-FOSSE

Downside Abbey, Stratton-on-the-Fosse, BA3 4RH
(01761) 235123   **w:** downside.co.uk

Open: By appointment only, please phone for details.

Description: Downside Abbey Church – the largest and
                 finest Neo-Gothic abbey in Britain.

Facilities: 🐕 ♿

Cameley St. James, Somerset

TEMPLE CLOUD

Cameley St James, Somerset, St James Church, Cameley,
Temple Cloud, BS39 5AH   **t:** (020) 7213 0660
: visitchurches.org.uk

Open: Daily, please phone for details.

Description: A delightfully unspoilt church, with a tower of
                 Mendip stone featuring a handsome parapet.
                 The interior has fixtures and fittings from
                 many periods and a wall painting of the Ten
                 Commandments.

Facilities: 🐕

Cleeve Abbey

WASHFORD

Cleeve Abbey, Washford, TA23 0PS
t: (01984) 640377   **w:** english-heritage.org.uk/cleeve

open: See website for details.
admission: £3.40

description: One of the few 13thC
monastic sites left with such a complete
set of cloister buildings.

facilities: 🏹 ⛱ ♿

Wells Cathedral

WELLS

Wells Cathedral, Chain Gate, Cathedral Green, Wells,
BA5 2UE   **t:** (01749) 674483   **w:** wellscathedral.org.uk

open: Apr-Sep, daily 0700-1900. Oct-Mar, daily
               0700-1800.
admission: £5.50

description: Dating from the 12th century and built in the
               Early English Gothic style.
               Magnificent west front
               with 296 medieval groups
               of sculpture. Chapter
               House and Lady Chapel.

facilities: ☕ 🏹 ♿

Rotherham Minster

ROTHERHAM

Rotherham Minster, All Saints Square, Rotherham, S60 1PW
t: (01709) 364737   **w:** rotherhamminster.org

open: All year, Mon-Tue, Thu-Fri, Sun 0900-1300
&1400-1600, Wed, Sat 0900-1200.

description: This site has been a place of worship since
Saxon times. The present Perpendicular-style
building is mainly 15th century although some
earlier structures remain. Don't miss the 16thC
roof bosses.

facilities:

Beauchief Abbey

SHEFFIELD

Beauchief Abbey, Beauchief Abbey Lane, Sheffield, S8 OEL
t: (0114) 221 1900

open: Please phone for details.

description: Attached to a 17thC church, only the abbey's
tower remains but is a beautiful example of
12thC architecture and a Scheduled Ancient
Monument. Medieval fishponds and ancient
woodland also remain.

facilities:

Sheffield Cathedral

Sheffield Cathedral, Church Street, Sheffield, S1 1HA
t: (0114) 275 3434 **w:** sheffield-cathedral.org.uk

open:	Mon-Fri 0845-1830, Sat 1000-1500, Sun 0800-1930. School Hols, Mon-Fri 0845-1700, Sat 1000-1500, Sun 0800-1930.
description:	There has been a church on this site since Saxon times. Rebuilt and modified over the centuries, history is written into its stones. Guided tours available.
facilities:	⚒ ♿

Saint Giles Church

St Giles Church, Charles Street, Cheadle, ST10 1NR
t: (01538) 753130 **w:** stgilescatholicchurch.co.uk

open:	All year, daily 0830-1630.
description:	A fine example of the work of the 19thC Gothic-revivalist architect and designer, AWN Pugin. Its 200ft spire dominates Cheadle and contains eight bells, six of which are original.
facilities:	⚒ ♿

Lichfield Cathedral

LICHFIELD

Lichfield Cathedral, The Visitors' Centre, The Close, Lichfield, WS13 7LD   **t:** (01543) 306240
w: lichfield-cathedral.org

open: All year, daily 0815-1815.

description: A medieval cathedral with three spires. See the 8thC Lichfield Gospels manuscript, superb 16thC Flemish glass, sculptures by Chantrey & Epstein and modern silver collection.

facilities:

Badley Saint Mary

BADLEY

Badley, St Mary, Badley, IP6 8RU
t: (020) 7213 0660   **w:** visitchurches.org.uk

open: Please contact keyholder for access..

description: The humble exterior of this building, dating in part from the Domesday Survey, gives no hint of the exquisite 17thC interior. Furnishings include medieval oak pews and benches, and Jacobean box pews. Also fine monuments.

facilities:

Saint Edmundsbury Cathedral

BURY ST EDMUNDS

Saint Edmundsbury Cathedral, The Cathedral Office, Angel Hill, Bury St Edmunds, IP33 1LS
t: (01284) 754933   **w:** stedscathedral.co.uk

open: Daily 0800-1800.

description: Come and see the magnificent Millennium Tower which now completes the last unfinished Anglican cathedral in England.

facilities: ☕ 🐾 ♿

Icklingham All Saints Church

ICKLINGHAM

Icklingham All Saints Church, The Hall Close, Icklingham, IP28 6PU   **t:** (020) 7213 0660   **w:** visitchurches.org.uk

open: Daily 1000-1600.

description: Dating largely from the 14th century, the quality of workmanship reflects the prosperity of the region at the time. The atmospheric interior has a fine arcade and cornices, elegant window tracery and excellent medieval stained glass.

facilities: 🐾 ♿

Little Wenham, All Saints

Little Wenham, All Saints, All Saints Church, Little Wenham,
CO7 6QA   t: (020) 7213 0660   w: visitchurches.org.uk

open: Please contact keyholder for access.

description: The exterior of this rural medieval church
                   has changed little since it was portrayed
                   by John Constable in 1798. Inside are what
                   Pevsner described as 'astonishingly good
                   wall paintings', good quality woodwork and
                   accomplished memorials.

facilities:

Holy Trinity Church

Holy Trinity Church, The Green, Long Melford, CO10 9DT
t: (01787) 310845   w: longmelfordchurch.com

open: Summer: daily 1000-1800. Winter: 1000-1700.

description: An almost entirely 15thC building. Only the
                   tower is modern, completed in 1903 as the
                   original was destroyed in a storm in 1710.
                   Don't miss the small medieval rabbit window.

facilities:

ALBURY

Albury St. Peter and St. Paul Church

Albury St Peter and St Paul Church, Albury Park, Albury, GU5 9BH   **t:** (020) 7213 0660   **w:** visitchurches.org.uk

open: Daily 1000-1600.

description: Delightful setting in Albury Park, this ancient church dates from Saxon and Norman times. Notable later additions include 18thC cupola over the tower, and Victorian mortuary chapel for Drummond family of Albury Park.

facilities:

GUILDFORD

Guildford Cathedral

Guildford Cathedral, Stag Hill, Guildford, GU2 7UP
t: (01483) 547860   **w:** guildford-cathedral.org

open: Daily 0830-1730. Tours: daily 0940-1600.

description: New Anglican cathedral, the foundation stone of which was laid in 1936. Notable sandstone interior and marble floors. Restaurant and shops.

facilities:

Saint Cuthbert's Church

St Cuthbert's Church, St Cuthberts Parish Centre, Market Place, Darlington, DL1 5QG   **t:** (01325) 358911

open: Apr-Oct 1100-1400.

description: Built in 1180, St Cuthbert's Darlington ('The Lady of the North') features 14thC belfry and font, 15thC misericords, 19thC stained glass and mosaic reredos.

facilities: 🏃 🛏 ♿

Gisborough Priory

Gisborough Priory, Church Street, Guisborough, TS14 6HG **t:** (01287) 633801   **w:** guisborough-town.com

open: Jan-Mar, Wed-Sun 0900-1700. Apr-Sep, Tue-Sun, Bank Hols 0900-1700. Oct-Dec, Wed-Sun, Bank Hols 0900-1700.

admission: £1.10

description: Remains of a priory founded by Robert de Brus in 1119. A priory for Augustinian canons in the grounds of Guisborough Hall. A sanctuary from busy market day shopping.

facilities: 🏃 🛏

Saint Hilda's Parish Church

St Hilda's Parish Church, The Headland, Hartlepool, TS24 0PW
t: (01429) 267030
w: hartlepool-sthilda.org.uk

open:	Apr-Sep, Sat-Sun, Wed 1400-1600. Oct-Mar, Sat 1400-1600.
description:	Magnificent early church giving views over the marina and Tees Bay. Fine tower with enormous buttresses, a splendid long nave and 7thC Saxon name stone.
facilities:	💺 🐕 🛆 ♿

Saint Cuthberts Church and Turner Mausoleum

St Cuthberts Church and Turner Mausoleum, 8 Keswick Road, Kirkleatham, Redcar, TS10 4JR
t: (01642) 485395

open:	Apr-Sep, Sat-Sun 1400-1700.

description: Georgian church (1763) and Turner mausoleum (1740) by James Gibbs. Important 17th and 18thC monuments and sculpture.

facilities: 🐕

Saint Pauls Monastery

Saint Pauls Monastery, Church Bank, Jarrow, NE32 3DZ
t: (01914) 897052

open: All year, Mon-Sat 100-1600, Sun 1430-1600.

description: Founded in 682, home of the Venerable Bede, re-founded in 1075. Remains of cloister buildings. Part of Bede's church survived as chancel of parish church.

facilities: 𝕏 ♿

Saint Nicholas Cathedral

St Nicholas Cathedral, St Nicholas Church Yard, Newcastle upon Tyne, NE1 1PF   t: (01912) 321939
w: newcastle-ang-cathedral-stnicholas.org.uk

open: All year, Mon-Fri 0700-1800, Sat 0830-1600, Sun 0700-1200 1600-1900, Bank Hols 0700-1200.

description: Thirteenth and 14thC church, added to in the 18thC-20thC. Famous lantern tower, pre-reformation font and font cover and 15thC stained glass roundel in the side chapel.

facilities: 💻 𝕏 ♿

Saint Andrew's Parish Church

SUNDERLAND

St Andrew's Parish Church, Talbot Road, Roker, Sunderland, SR6 9PT   **t:** (01915) 160135
w: monkwearmouthparish.co.uk

open: All year, Mon-Fri 0900-1300.

description: A 20thC church by E S Prior. Arts and crafts interior with mural by Macdonald Gill. Furnishings by Gimson, Burne-Jones, Morris, Randal Wells and Payne.

facilities:

Saint Peters' Church

SUNDERLAND

St Peters' Church, St Peters Way, Sunderland, SR6 0DY
t: (01915) 160135   **w:** monkwearmouthparish.co.uk

open: Apr-Sep, 1000-1200. 1400-1600.

description: Saxon tower, west wall and stones of major archaeological importance. Bede spent his early years here.

facilities:

Tynemouth Castle and Priory

TYNEMOUTH

Tynemouth Castle and Priory, Tynemouth, NE30 4BZ
t: (01912) 571090   **w:** english-heritage.org.uk

open: See website for details.
admission: £3.40

description: Dating from the 7th century, the burial place of Northumbrian kings. The priory was destroyed by the Danes, later founded as a Benedictine Priory, and is now a picturesque ruin.

facilities: 🐕 ⛱ ♿

Holy Trinity Church

OLD TOWN

Holy Trinity Church, The Parish Office, Old Town, CV37 6BG
t: (01789) 266316   **w:** stratford-upon-avon.org

open: Apr-Sep, daily 0830-1800. Oct, Daily 0900-1700. Nov-Feb,Daily 0900-1600. Mar, Daily 0900-1700.

description: Set on banks of the river Avon, the parish church is often described as one of England's most beautiful. Contains the graves of William Shakespeare and family.

facilities: 🍴 ⛱ ♿

Collegiate Church of St Mary

Collegiate Church of St Mary, Old Square, Warwick, CV34 4RA   **t:** (01926) 400771   **w:** stmaryswarwick.org.uk

open:	Apr-Oct, daily 1000-1800. Nov-Mar, daily 1000-1630.
admission:	£1.00
description:	Famous for its incomparable 15thC Beauchamp Chapel with superb glass and medieval/Tudor tombs. Norman crypt, 14thC chancel and chapter house.
facilities:	犬 宀 ಕ

Birmingham Cathedral (St Philips)

Birmingham Cathedral (St Philips), Colmore Row, Birmingham, B3 2QB   **t:** (0121) 262 1840

open:	Apr-Jul, Mon-Fri 0800-1800, Sat 0930-1600, Sun 0900-1730. Aug, Mon-Sun 0800-1600. Sep-Mar, Mon-Fri 0800-1800, Sat 0930-1600, Sun 0900-1730.
description:	A beautiful historic building at the heart of the city, Birmingham Cathedral contains four famous Pre-Raphaelite windows by Burne-Jones, surrounded by a restored churchyard.
facilities:	犬 ಕ

Saint Chad's Cathedral

BIRMINGHAM

St Chad's Cathedral, Queensway, Birmingham, B4 6EU
: (0121) 236 2251   **w:** stchadscathedral.org.uk

open: All year, Mon-Fri 0800-1700, Sat 0900-1700,
                  Sun, Bank Hols 0900-1300.

description: A Gothic-style cathedral with German or
                  Belgian influences - notably fine twin spires.
                  Also 15thC German and Flemish artwork and
                  excellent John Hardman stained glass.

facilities: 🐕

Coventry Cathedral

COVENTRY

Coventry Cathedral, Priory Street, Coventry, CV1 5ES
: (024) 7652 1200   **w:** coventrycathedral.org.uk

open: Daily 0900-1700.
admission: £3.50

description: Glorious 20thC
                  cathedral rising above
                  the stark ruins of the
                  medieval cathedral
                  destroyed in 1940.
                  The visitor centre
                  includes audio-visual
                  shows.

facilities: ☕ 🏃 ♿

Priory Visitor Centre

COVENTRY

Priory Visitor Centre, Priory Row, Coventry, CV1 5EX
t: (024) 7655 2242   **w:** theherbert.org

open:	All year, Mon-Sat 1000-1700, Sun 1200-1600.
description:	Opened in August 2001, the Visitor Centre tells the story of Coventry's first cathedral from the time of Lady Godiva to the 16th century.
facilities:	犬 卅 ᵔ

Cathedral of Our Lady and St Philip Howard

ARUNDEL

Cathedral of Our Lady and St Philip Howard, London Road, Arundel, BN18 9AY   **t:** (01903) 882297
w: arundelcathedral.org

open:	Apr-Oct, daily 0900-1800. Nov-Mar, daily 0900-dusk.
description:	A Roman Catholic cathedral built by hansom cab inventor, A J Hansom. Consecrated in 1965. Shrine of St Philip Howard. Sussex wrought ironwork. Limewood statue.
facilities:	犬 ᵔ

North Stoke Church

ARUNDEL

North Stoke Church, North Stoke, Arundel, BN18 9LS
(020) 7213 0660   **w:** visitchurches.org.uk

Open: Daily 1000-1600.

description: Idyllically situated on the South Downs, this cruciform church of simple and elegant proportions is virtually unaltered since medieval times, giving an impression of height and space. Early stained glass and fine stone carving.

Facilities: 🐕 ♿

Warminghurst, The Holy Sepluchre

ASHINGTON

Warminghurst, The Holy Sepluchre, Rectory Lane, Ashington,
RH20 3AP   **t:** (020) 7213 0660   **w:** visitchurches.org.uk

Open: Daily 1000-1600.

Description: This simple 13thC sandstone building enjoys splendid views across the South Downs. It has a wonderfully unspoilt 18thC interior, with an elegant three-arched screen dividing nave from chancel, together with excellent furnishings.

Facilities: 🐕

Saint Wilfrids Chapel

BOGNOR REGIS

St Wilfrid's Chapel, Harbour Road, Church Norton, Bognor Regis, PO21 4TD t: (020) 7213 0660
w: visitchurches.org.uk

open: Daily 1100-1600.

description: The 13thC chancel of a Norman church rebuilt in Selsey in the 19th century. Contains magnificent 1537 monument to John and Agas Lewis. Vivid carving of martyrdom of St Agnes. Interesting modern stained glass.

facilities:

Chichester Cathedral

CHICHESTER

Chichester Cathedral, West Street, Chichester, PO19 1PX
t: (01243) 782595
w: chichestercathedral.org.uk

open: Apr-Oct, daily 0715-1900. Nov-Mar, daily 0715-1800.

description: Mainly Norman architecture. Detached bell tower, Sutherland painting, Chagall window, Skelton font, modern tapestries. Site of the Shrine of St Richard. Romanesque stone carvings.

facilities:

Chichester, St John the Evangelist Chapel

Chichester, St John the Evangelist Chapel, St Johns Street, Chichester, PO19 1UR   **t:** (020) 7213 0660
w: visitchurches.org.uk

open: Daily 1000-1600.

description: A rare and almost unchanged example of an evangelical preaching house. The layout of the interior reflects the importance placed on sermons and reading from scripture.

facilities: 🎨 ♿

Lancing College Chapel

Lancing College Chapel, Lancing College, Lancing, BN15 0RW   **t:** (01273) 452213   **w:** lancingcollege.co.uk

open: All year, Mon-Sat 1000-1600, Sun 1200-1600.

description: Lancing College Chapel was built in 13thC Gothic style from 1868 and dedicated in 1911. The 32ft rose window is one of the largest in England.

facilities: 🎨 🍽 ♿

Tortington St Mary Magdalene

Tortington St Mary Magdalene, Ford Road, Tortington, BN18 0FD   **t:** (020) 7213 0660   **w:** visitchurches.org.uk

open: Daily 1000-1600.

description: Outwardly, this picturesque two-cell Norman church is little changed from when built to serve the lay tenants of Tortington Priory. Inside, the exceptional Caen stone chancel arch has intricate beak heads and and grotesques.

facilities: 🐕

Bradford Cathedral

Bradford Cathedral, 1 Stott Hill, Bradford, BD1 4EH   **t:** (01274) 777720   **w:** bradfordcathedral.co.uk

open: Daily 0800-1800.

description: Bradford's beautiful cathedral is a hidden jewel. Set in tranquil gardens where once battle raged, the cathedral is alive with a sense of history from its 13 centuries at the heart of the city..

facilities: 🧗 ⛱ ♿

Dewsbury Minster

Dewsbury Minster, Rishworth Road, Dewsbury, WF12 8DD
t: (01924) 465491

open: All year, Mon-Sat 0930-1530.

description: Refectory serving food
and drinks, heritage centre
containing information on the
long history of the minster
as part of the Church of England since St
Paulinus in AD 627.

facilities:

Harewood All Saints

Harewood All Saints, Castlewood Close, Harewood,
LS17 9LG   **t:** (0113) 218 1010   **w:** harewood.org

open: Mar-Oct, Daily 1000-1630

description: Set within the park of Harewood House, the
church was much restored in the 1860s. Its six
alabaster tombs offer a unique history of the
development of alabaster carving.

facilities:

Church of St Peter and St Leonard

HORBURY

The Church of St Peter and St Leonard, Horbury, WF4 6LT
t: (01924) 271710   **w:** horburyvillage.com

open: Daily 0900-1200.

description: Widely held to be the finest Georgian church
in West Yorkshire, St Peter and St Leonard
dates from 1791-1793 and was designed by
architect John Carr.

facilities:

Kirkstall Abbey

KIRKSTALL

Kirkstall Abbey, Abbey Road, Kirkstall, LS5 3EH
t: (0113) 247 8391   **w:** leeds.gov.uk

open: Daily, dawn-dusk.

description: One of the best-preserved medieval Cistercian
monasteries in the country. Constructed
between 1152 and 1182, many of its buildings
still survive virtually intact up to eaves level.

facilities:

All Saints Church

PONTEFRACT

All Saints Church, Ackton Lane, Featherstone, Pontefract,
WF7 6AR   **t:** (01977)792280   **w:** wakefield.anglican.org

open: Daily.

description: An interesting Grade II* Listed church of
                   medieval origin with parts of the building
                   dating from the 12th century.

facilities: 🐕 ♿

Saint Giles' Church

PONTEFRACT

St Giles' Church, Market Place, Pontefract, WF8 1AT
t: (01977) 706803   **w:** stgilesonline.org.uk

open: All year, Mon-Fri 1000-1500, Sat 0900-1300.

description: Standing prominently in the market place, St
                   Giles' octagonal bell and clock tower is visible
                   from most approaches to the town.

facilities: ☕ 🐕 🪑 ♿

365 Churches, Abbeys and Cathedrals

SALTAIRE

Saltaire United Reformed Church

Saltaire United Reformed Church, Victoria Road, Saltaire, BD18 3LA   **t:** (01274) 597894   **w:** saltaireurc.org.uk

open: Apr-Sep, daily 1400-1600. Oct-Mar, Sun 1400-1600.

description: Built by Sir Titus Salte in 1859, this Grade I Listed building is a unique example of Italianate religious architecture. Features a fretted tower with cupola and an ornate interior.

facilities:

WAKEFIELD

Saint Austin's Catholic Church

St Austin's Catholic Church, Wentworth Terrace, Wakefield, WF1 3QN   **t:** (01924) 372080   **w:** staustins.co.uk

open: Daily 0800-1300.

description: Pre-dating Catholic emancipation, St Austins is one of the few Georgian era Catholic churches still in regular use for worship.

facilities:

Saint Catherine's Church

St Catherine's Church, Doncaster Road, Belle Vue, Wakefield,
WF1 5HL **t:** (01924) 211130 **w:** the-co-op.com

open: All year, Mon-Fri 0900-1700.

description: An excellent example of a modern church
heavily influenced by the Liturgical Movement
and designed as the House of the People of
God.

facilities: ▆ ⚒ ♿

Church of St John the Baptist

The Church of St John the Baptist, St John's Square,
Wentworth Street, Wakefield, WF1 2QU
t: (01924) 371029 **w:** wakefield-stjohns.org.uk

open: All year, Wed 1000-1300, Sun 0800-0830,
1000-1200.

description: Set within a landscaped square, this attractive
Grade II* Listed church forms the centrepiece
of Wakefields Georgian town development.

facilities: ▆ ⚒ ⛩ ♿

Wakefield Cathedral

WAKEFIELD

Wakefield Cathedral, Northgate, Wakefield, WF1 1HG
t: (01924) 373923

open: All year, Mon-Fri 0830-1750, Sat 0830-1600.

 description: The present building dates mainly from the 14th and 15th centuries. Perpendicular style, with the tallest spire in Yorkshire. Restored by George Gilbert Scott and featuring a fine set of Kempe stained glass windows.

facilities: 🐾 ♿

Westgate Chapel (Unitarian)

WAKEFIELD

Westgate Chapel (Unitarian), Westgate, Wakefield, WF1 1XR
t: (01924) 372748

open: By appointment only, please phone for details.

description: Grade II* Listed Georgian chapel dating from 1752. Leading industrialists, innovators, members of Parliament and political radicals are among those who are interred in its catacombs.

facilities: 🐾 ♿

Church of St Michael and Our Lady

WRAGBY

The Church of St Michael and Our Lady, Nostell Priory, Wragby, WF4 1QX   t: (01977) 610497   w: wragby.org.uk

open: All year, daily 0900-1700.

description: Set within the grounds of Nostell Priory this is truly a hidden gem. Built in Perpendicular style during the reign of Henry VIII.

facilities: 🐕 ♿

Fisherton Delamere, St. Nicholas

FISHERTON DE LA MERE

Fisherton Delamere, St Nicholas, Fisherton De La Mere, BA12 0PZ   t: (020) 7213 0660   w: visitchurches.org.uk

open: Daily 0900-1700.

description: The exterior of this 14thC church is constructed in a chequerboard pattern of flint and stone. Substantially reconstructed in the 19thC, it has an elegant Edwardian screen separating nave and chancel, and interesting monuments.

facilities: 🍽

Inglesham St. John the Baptist

Inglesham St John the Baptist, Inglesham, SN6 7RD
t: (020) 7213 0660   **w:** visitchurches.org.uk

open:	Daily 0900-1700.
description:	A church of Saxon origin with a powerful Saxon carving and seven centuries of wall paintings. The interior is much as it would have been in the 17th century.
facilities:	

Lacock Abbey

Lacock Abbey, Lacock, SN15 2LG
t: (01249) 730227   **w:** nationaltrust.org.uk

open:	Apr-Oct, Mon, Wed-Sun 1300-1730.
admission:	£6.30
description:	Founded in the 13thC and dissolved in 1539 since when it has been the home of the Talbot family. Medieval cloisters, 18thC Gothic hall and 16thC stable court.
facilities:	

Malmesbury Abbey

Malmesbury Abbey, Parish Office,
The Old Squash Court, Malmesbury,
SN16 0AA   t: (01666) 826666
w: malmesburyabbey.com

open: Daily 1000-1600.

description: Norman/Romanesque abbey, now the parish
church. Founded by St Aldhelm in Saxon
times c676.

facilities: 🐕 ♿

Saint Peter's Church, Marlborough

St Peter's Church, Marlborough, High Street, Marlborough,
SN8 1HQ   t: (01672) 511453

open: All year, Mon-Sat 1000-1700, Bank Hols 1100-
1600.

description: Permanent art and crafts display, coffee and
snacks in an historic redundant church.

facilities: ☕ 🐕 ♿

Salisbury Cathedral

SALISBURY

Salisbury Cathedral, Visitor Services, 33 The Close, Salisbury, SP1 2EJ **t:** (01722) 555120
w: salisburycathedral.org.uk

open: Daily 0715-1815. 11 Jun-24 Aug, Mon-Sat, late opening until 1915.
admission: £5.00

description: Britain's finest 13thC Gothic cathedral. Discover nearly 800 years of history, including Britain's tallest spire, the world's best preserved Magna Carta (AD1215) and Europe's oldest working clock (AD1386).

facilities:

Saint Cassian's Church

CHADDESLEY CORBETT

St Cassian's Church, Chaddesley Corbett, DY10 4SA
t: (01527) 831809

open: Jan-Dec, daily 0800-2000.

description: Largely of Norman foundation, dating from 12thC, the church features architecture and monuments of great historical interest.

facilities:

See pages 2-3 for key to symbols

Great Witley Parish Church

GREAT WITLEY

Great Witley Parish Church, Witley Court Drive, Great Witley, WR6 6JT **t:** (01299) 896406

open: Daily 1000-1700.

description: Baroque church famous for gilded stucco, painted ceiling and enamelled windows.

facilities: ▆ ✗ ♿

Saint Mary and All Saints Church

KIDDERMINSTER

St Mary and All Saints Church, Churchfields, Kidderminster, DY10 2JN **t:** (01562) 751923 **w:** kpctm.co.uk

open: All year, Tue-Fri 1100-1500. Or contact office.

description: The largest parish church in Worcestershire, buildings dating from the 16th century. Richard Baxter was a preacher here. Fine tombs, glass, organ and bell tower.

facilities: ✗ ♿

Little Malvern Priory

Little Malvern Priory, Little Malvern, WR14 4JN
t: (01684) 567439   w: littlemalvernpriory.co.uk

open: All year.

description: A Benedictine priory, partly demolished, now
              the local parish church.

facilities: 🐕 ⛉ ♿

Great Malvern Priory Church

Great Malvern Priory Church, Parish Office, Church Street,
Malvern, WR14 2AY   t: (01684) 561020
w: greatmalvernpriory.org.uk

open: Daily 0900-1700.

description: A Benedictine foundation priory church of
              early Norman (1085) and Perpendicular
              architecture containing 15thC glass medieval
              encaustic tiles and misericords.

facilities: 🖥 🐕 ⛉ ♿

Pershore Abbey

Pershore Abbey, Church Street, Pershore, WR10 1DT
(01386) 561520   w: pershoreabbey.fsnet.co.uk

open: Apr-Oct, Mon-Sat 0800-1700. Nov-Mar, Mon-Sat 0800-1600.

description: Ancient abbey church with Norman crossing, 13thC chancel with decorated vault, rare triforium with clerestory, and fine lantern tower with unique ringing platform.

facilities: 🚶 ⛩ ♿

Croome D'Abitot, St Mary Magdalene

Croome D'Abitot, St Mary Magdalene, Croome D'Abitot, Severn Stoke, WR8 9DW   t: (020) 7213 0660
w: visitchurches.org.uk

open: All year, Thu-Mon 1100-1700.

description: Designed by Robert Adam and Capability Brown as an 'eyecatcher' in Croome Park for the 6th Earl of Coventry, the church is an excellent example of fantastic 'Gothick' style. Magnificent monuments to Earls of Coventry.

facilities: 🐕

Worcester Cathedral

WORCESTER

Worcester Cathedral, 10a College Green, Worcester,
WR1 2LH   **t:** (01905) 611002   **w:** cofe-worcester.org.uk

open: All year, Mon-Sat 0730-1800, Sun 0730-1830.
admission: £3.00

description: One of England's loveliest
cathedrals with medieval
cloisters, an ancient crypt and
Chapter House and magnificent
Victorian stained glass.

facilities: